LOTTERY FUNDED
Supported using public funding by
ARTS COUNCIL ENGLAND

Front cover: Carlos Acosta as Basilio in his own production of *Don Quixote* ©ROH/Johan Persson, 2013

Inside front cover: Artists of The Royal Ballet in Christopher Wheeldon's *The Winter's Tale* ©ROH/Johan Persson, 2014

Inside back cover: Artists of The Royal Ballet in Frederick Ashton's *Rhapsody* ©ROH/Johan Persson, 2014

Back cover: Artists of The Royal Ballet in Alastair Marriott's *Connectome* ©ROH/Bill Cooper, 2014

Opposite: Portrait of Kevin O'Hare ©Joe Plimmer

First published in 2014 by the Royal Opera House
in association with Oberon Books Ltd
Oberon Books Ltd
521 Caledonian Road, London N7 9RH
Tel +44 (0)20 7607 3637
info@oberonbooks.com
www.oberonbooks.com

Cover and book design: James Illman

Editor: Andrew Walby

For the Royal Opera House:

Commissioning Editor: John Snelson

Project Manager: Will Richmond

Content Production Assistant: Nicholas Manderson

Additional contributor: Gerard Davis

Every effort has been made to trace the copyright holders of all images reprinted in this book. Acknowledgement is made in all cases where the image source is available, but we would be grateful for information about any images where sources could not be traced.

A catalogue record for this book is available from the British Library.

ISBN 978-1-78319-081-2

Printed and bound by
CPI Group (UK) Ltd, Croydon, CR0 4YY

Royal Opera House
Covent Garden
London WC2E 9DD
Box Office +44 (0)20 7304 4000
www.roh.org.uk

We are very much looking forward to our 2014/15 Season, which is filled with classics and groundbreaking new work, both on the main stage and in the Linbury Studio Theatre. The range of choreography and the fine talents of the dancers on show this Season really represent the very best of everything that makes The Royal Ballet what it is today.

This Season The Royal Ballet is also particularly proud to have been awarded the Queen Elizabeth II Coronation Award, the highest honour awarded by the Royal Academy of Dance. Inaugurated 60 years ago and given in recognition of outstanding services to ballet, its first recipient was our own Founder, Ninette de Valois.

In this book you will find a preview of the Season ahead as well as a selection of the best photographs of the ballets presented in the 2013/14 Season. Articles look at Ballet Healthcare – a crucial aspect of a dancer's training and maintenance – and Stage Management – the team that makes sure everything runs smoothly for every performance.

I do hope you continue to enjoy the tremendous variety of our work, the versatility and theatricality of our fantastic dancers and choreographers, and the many creative artists who will be working with us throughout the coming year.

Kevin O'Hare
Director, The Royal Ballet

2014/15 SEASON PREVIEW

HERITAGE WORKS

This Season Kenneth MacMillan's *Manon* celebrates its 40th year in the repertory. What better way to open this 2014/15 Royal Ballet Season than with this world-famous classic and signature work of the Company. The revival will feature a number of exciting debuts in the principal roles including, as Manon, Francesca Hayward (opposite Edward Watson's Des Grieux), Melissa Hamilton partnered by Matthew Golding, and Vadim Muntagirov in his debut as Des Grieux (opposite Lauren Cuthbertson). Carlos Acosta returns in the role of Des Grieux and will also make his debut as Lescaut. *Manon* also opens the Royal Opera House Live Cinema Season, with the performance on 16 October broadcast live into cinemas worldwide.

The mixed programme that follows continues the heritage works this Season with a programme of four treasured shorter ballets by the Company's Founder Choreographer Frederick Ashton. These will be the abstract masterpieces *Symphonic Variations* and *Scènes de ballet*, the exquisite narrative miniature *A Month in the Country* and the bold, carefree *Five Brahms Waltzes in the Manner of Isadora Duncan*, performed by Lauren Cuthbertson.

There is more MacMillan with his powerful and harrowing *Song of the Earth* in a mixed programme with two ballets by Jerome Robbins – the first revival of *In the Night* since it was re-introduced to the repertory in the 2012/13 Season, and Robbins's sensual, dreamlike *Afternoon of a Faun*. Ashton's joyous, full-Company ballet *La Fille mal gardée* will be performed in the Spring.

Another favourite of the repertory – John Cranko's gorgeous, tragic *Onegin* – will be revived in January, allowing several of the Company's finest dance-actors to take on the defining roles of this drama.

NEW WORKS AND CONTEMPORARY REVIVALS

The 2014/15 Season will also feature new works from a range of cutting-edge choreographers and a number of contemporary revivals.

Royal Ballet Resident Choreographer Wayne McGregor will create his first full-length ballet on the Company. The inspiration for *Woolf Works*, which will be given its premiere in May, comes from the life and writing of Virginia Woolf and her most famous character, Mrs Dalloway. McGregor's choreography will be set to a specially commissioned score from acclaimed British composer Max Richter (McGregor previously collaborated with Richter on *Sum* and *Infra*).

An exciting programme of 21st-century ballets presents two works recently created for the Company and one world premiere. Artist in Residence Liam Scarlett's *The Age of Anxiety*, based on W.H. Auden's Pulitzer Prize-winning 1947 poem, set to Leonard Bernstein's Symphony no.2, which was also inspired by the poem, will be given its premiere in November.

The Age of Anxiety will appear alongside Artistic Associate Christopher Wheeldon's Olivier Award-winning *Aeternum* and Kim Brandstrup's *Ceremony of Innocence* – an impressionistic, elegiac

Opposite page: Roberta Marquez as Manon and Steven McRae as Des Grieux in MacMillan's *Manon*

©ROH/Johan Persson, 2011

This page:

Top: Portrait of Virginia Woolf (1882-1941), published by Editions Stock / Private Collection / Archives Charmet / Bridgeman Images

Bottom: W.H. Auden on Fire Island, New York, August 1946

©Jerry Cooke/ Corbis

This Page:
Poster for Deloitte Ignite 14

Opposite page:
Left to right:
Luca Acri, Francesca Hayward and Marcelino Sambé in Christopher Wheeldon's *The Winter's Tale*
©ROH/Johan Persson, 2014

work created for the 2013 Aldeburgh Festival as part of the global celebrations to mark the centenary of Benjamin Britten's birth.

This Season includes a new full-Company work by guest choreographer Hofesh Shechter, winner of the 2008 Critics' Circle Award for Best Choreography (Modern). Shechter will bring his thrilling, politicized dance language to the Royal Opera House for the first time as part of a mixed programme that will also include Balanchine's radiant 20th century classic *The Four Temperaments*.

Two recent additions to the Company repertory – Wheeldon's *Alice's Adventures in Wonderland* and Carlos Acosta's *Don Quixote* – will be revived over the Christmas period. No Season would be complete without at least one of the big classic favourites – this February it will be Anthony Dowell's *Swan Lake*. *Swan Lake* will be relayed around the world as part of the Royal Opera House Live Cinema Season, which will also include *La Fille mal gardée* and *Alice's Adventures in Wonderland*.

THE ROYAL BALLET STUDIO PROGRAMME

This Season The Royal Ballet takes control of the Deloitte Ignite festival. Deloitte Ignite 14 opens the Season in September, co-curated by the National Gallery's Minna Moore Ede, provoking a host of creative responses to the notion of myth and bringing together dance, art, film, storytelling, yoga and much more. The festival focuses especially on the myths of Prometheus and his theft of fire, and Leda and her encounter with Zeus in the form of a swan. Opening the festival are three performances of *Sampling the Myth* – a programme of dance and film, including classic *pas de deux* and solos, a *pas de deux* from Matthew Bourne's *Swan Lake* and a new piece by Aakash Odedra, as well as dance films by Kim Brandstrup, Robert Binet and Charlotte Edmonds. All-male dance group BalletBoyz theTALENT perform ten shows in the Linbury Studio Theatre in September.

New dance includes works from ZooNation (*The Madhatter's Tea Party*, which runs in parallel with *Alice's Adventures in Wonderland* on the main stage), Ludovic Ondiviela (*Cassandra*), Aakash Odedra, Shobana Jeyasingh and Wendy Whelan. In February, we welcome back Draft Works – The Royal Ballet's annual platform for Company dancers and invited guests to experiment with choreographic sketches. Visiting companies include Phoenix Dance Theatre, which returns with works by Darshan Singh Bhuller, Ivgi & Greben and a new work by Christopher Bruce. Other regular appearances in the studio programme include the return of Ballet Black, for their fourteenth Season in the Linbury, the London International Mime Festival, Northern Ballet and the now annual 'Springboard', a showcase for international youth companies.

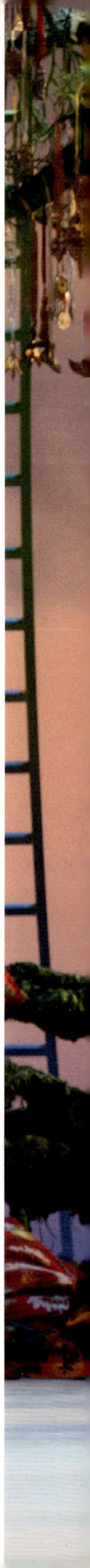

PROMOTIONS, ENTRANCES AND EXITS

Matthew Golding, formerly Principal dancer with the Dutch National Ballet, joined the Company as Principal in January 2014.

Vadim Muntagirov, former Principal with English National Ballet, joined the Company as Principal in March 2014.

For the 2014/15 Season, Akane Takada and Valentino Zucchetti are promoted to First Soloist.

Francesca Hayward, Yasmine Naghdi, Tristan Dyer and Fernando Montaño are all promoted to Soloists, and Jacqueline Clark, Elsa Godard, Gemma Pitchley-Gale, Luca Acri, Nicol Edmonds, Kevin Emerton and Marcelino Sambé, are all promoted to First Artists.

During the 2013/14 Season Matthew Ball, Reece Clarke, Gina Storm-Jensen (all graduates of The Royal Ballet School) and Isabella Gasparini joined the Company as Artists. Also joining as Artists in the new Season are Royal Ballet School alumni Calvin Richardson, Hannah Grennell (from Dutch National Ballet) and Mariko Sasaki (from Birmingham Royal Ballet).

Joining the Company as part of the new Aud Jebsen Young Dancers Programme for the 2014/15 Season are Grace Blundell and Grace Horler, both from The Royal Ballet School, Ashley Scott and Ashleigh McKimmie from English National Ballet School and Maria Barroso from Semperoper Ballet, Dresden.

David Yudes joins the Company as Prix de Lausanne Dancer for the 2014/15 Season.

At the end of the 2013/14 Season Soloist Kenta Kura retired from the Company after 17 years to begin a new appointment as Boys' Artistic Teacher at The Royal Ballet School, White Lodge. Kenta is a graduate of the Professional Dancers' Teachers Course (PDTC) at The Royal Ballet School.

First Artist Leanne Cope will take a sabbatical for the 2014/15 Season to play the part of Lise Dassin in *An American in Paris*, directed and choreographed by Christopher Wheeldon, Artistic Associate of The Royal Ballet.

Soloist Iohna Loots left the Company during the 2013/14 Season, First Artist Sabina Westcombe and Artists Ruth Bailey and Claudia Dean also left the Company at the end of the Season.

THE 2014/15 SEASON AT A GLANCE

This page:
Left to right:
Emma Maguire as Vera and Rupert Pennefather as Baliaev in *A Month in the Country*
©ROH/Tristram Kenton, 2012
Sarah Lamb in *Afternoon of a Faun*
©ROH/Dee Conway, 2008
Itziar Mendizabal and Alexander Campbell in *Ceremony of Innocence*
©Rob Marrison
Artists of The Royal Ballet in *Scènes de Ballet*
©ROH/Johan Persson, 2011

Opposite page:
Left to right:
Nehemiah Kish and Zenaida Yanowsky in *In the Night*
©ROH/Tristram Kenton, 2012
Artists of The Royal Ballet in *Onegin*
©ROH/Bill Cooper, 2010

SEPTEMBER/OCTOBER

MANON
Choreography Kenneth MacMillan
Music Jules Massenet
orchestrated by Martin Yates
Originally compiled by Leighton Lucas
with the collaboration of Hilda Gaunt

Designs Nicholas Georgiadis
Lighting design John B. Read

THURSDAY 16 OCTOBER

MANON
Live in cinemas

OCTOBER

SCÈNES DE BALLET
Choreography Frederick Ashton
Music Igor Stravinsky

Designs André Beaurepaire
Lighting design John B. Read

FIVE BRAHMS WALTZES IN THE MANNER OF ISADORA DUNCAN
Choreography Frederick Ashton
Music Johannes Brahms

Costume designs David Dean

SYMPHONIC VARIATIONS
Choreography Frederick Ashton
Music César Franck

Set and costume designs
Sophie Fedorovitch
Lighting design John B. Read

A MONTH IN THE COUNTRY
Choreography Frederick Ashton
Music Fryderyk Chopin
arranged by John Lanchbery

Designs Julia Trevelyan Oman
Lighting design William Bundy
re-created by John Charlton

OCTOBER/NOVEMBER

CASSANDRA
Choreography Ludovic Ondiviela
Music Ana Silvera

Filming Director Kate Church

NOVEMBER

CEREMONY OF INNOCENCE
Choreography Kim Brandstrup
Music Benjamin Britten

Costume designs Kandis Cook
Designs Leo Warner for 59 Productions
Lighting design Jordan Tuinman

THE AGE OF ANXIETY
Choreography Liam Scarlett
Music Leonard Bernstein

Designs John MacFarlane
Lighting design Jennifer Tipton

AETERNUM
Choreography Christopher Wheeldon
Music Benjamin Britten

Designs Jean-Marc Puissant
Lighting design Adam Silverman

NOVEMBER/DECEMBER/JANUARY

DON QUIXOTE
Choreography and production
Carlos Acosta *after* Marius Petipa
Music Ludwig Minkus *arranged and orchestrated by* Martin Yates

Designs Tim Hatley
Lighting design Hugh Vanstone

DECEMBER/JANUARY

ALICE'S ADVENTURES IN WONDERLAND
Choreography Christopher Wheeldon
Music Joby Talbot

Designs Bob Crowley
Scenario Nicholas Wright
Lighting design Natasha Katz
Projection design Jon Driscoll
and Gemma Carrington

TUESDAY 16 DECEMBER

ALICE'S ADVENTURES IN WONDERLAND
Live in Cinemas

THE MAD HATTER'S TEA PARTY
Choreography and Director Kate Prince
Music Josh Cohen *and* DJ Wade

Set design Ben Stones

JANUARY

MURMUR/INKED

Choreography Aakash Odedra, Lewis Major/Damien Jalet
Music Nicki Wells/Loscil

Costume designs (Inked) Jean Paul Lespagnard
Lighting design Andrew Ellis/Fabbiana Piccioli

JANUARY/FEBRUARY

ONEGIN

Choreography John Cranko
Music Kurt-Heinz Stolze
After Pytor Il'yich Tchaikovsky

Designs Jürgen Rose *after original 1969 designs for Stuttgart Ballet*
Lighting design Steen Bjarke

FEBRUARY

DRAFT WORKS

FEBRUARY/MARCH

SWAN LAKE

Choreography Marius Petipa *and* Lev Ivanov
Additional Choreography by Frederick Ashton *and* David Bintley
Music Pytor Il'yich Tchaikovsky

Production Anthony Dowell
Designs Yolanda Sonnabend
Lighting design Mark Henderson

TUESDAY 17 MARCH

SWAN LAKE
Live in Cinemas

MARCH

NEW SHOBANA JEYASINGH

Choreography Shobana Jeyasingh
Music Gabriel Prokofiev

MARCH/APRIL

THE FOUR TEMPERAMENTS

Choreography George Balanchine
Music Paul Hindemith

Lighting design John B. Read

NEW HOFESH SHECHTER

Choreography Hofesh Shechter

SONG OF THE EARTH

Choreography Kenneth MacMillan
Music Gustav Mahler

Designs Nicholas Georgiadis
Lighting design John B. Read

APRIL/MAY

LA FILLE MAL GARDÉE

Choreography Frederick Ashton
Music Ferdinand Hérold *arranged and orchestrated by* John Lanchbery

Scenario Jean Dauberval
Designs Osbert Lancaster
Lighting design John B. Read

TUESDAY 5 MAY

LA FILLE MAL GARDÉE
Live in cinemas

MAY

WOOLF WORKS

Choreography and Director Wayne McGregor
Music Max Richter

Designs Wayne McGregor
Costume designs Moritz Junge
Lighting design Lucy Carter
Film design Ravi Deepres
Dramaturg Uzma Hammed

MAY/JUNE

AFTERNOON OF A FAUN

Choreography Jerome Robbins
Music Claude Debussy

Original set and lighting design Jean Rosenthal
Lighting re-created by Les Dickert
Costume designs Irene Sharaff

IN THE NIGHT

Choreography Jerome Robbins
Music Fryderyk Chopin

Costume designs Anthony Dowell
Lighting Jennifer Tipton *re-created by* Les Dickert

SONG OF THE EARTH

Choreography Kenneth MacMillan
Music Gustav Mahler

Designs Nicholas Georgiadis
Lighting design John B. Read

DON QUIXOTE

Opposite page: Laura Morera as Mercedes and Ryoichi Hirano as Espada

This page:

Top: Artists of The Royal Ballet

Bottom: Christopher Saunders as Don Quixote and Philip Mosley as Sancho Panza

©ROH/Johan Persson, 2013

ROMEO AND JULIET

Opposite page: Steven McRae as Romeo and Artists of The Royal Ballet

This page: Natalia Osipova as Juliet

©ROH/Johan Persson, 2013

CHROMA

Opposite page: Olivia Cowley and Edward Watson

This page: Lauren Cuthbertson and Eric Underwood

THE HUMAN SEASONS

Opposite page: Marianela Nuñez and Federico Bonelli

This page: Melissa Hamilton and Steven McRae

©ROH/Bill Cooper, 2013

THE RITE OF SPRING

Claudia Dean as The Chosen Maiden and Artists of The Royal Ballet

©ROH/Bill Cooper, 2013

THE NUTCRACKER

Opposite Page: Francesca Hayward as Clara

This Page: Meaghan Grace Hinkis as Clara

JEWELS

Opposite page:

Top: Natalia Osipova and Artists of The Royal Ballet in 'Rubies'

Bottom: Artists of The Royal Ballet in 'Diamonds'

This page: Akane Takada in 'Emeralds'

HANSEL AND GRETEL

This page:

Left: Kristen McNally as Mother

Right: Elizabeth Harrod as Gretel and Donald Thom as the Sandman

Opposite page: Ryoichi Hirano as the Witch and Donald Thom as the Sandman

©ROH/Tristram Kenton, 2013

GISELLE

Carlos Acosta as Count Albrecht and Hikaru Kobayashi as Myrtha, with Artists of The Royal Ballet

©ROH/Bill Cooper, 2014

RHAPSODY

Opposite page:
Yuhui Choe

This page:
James Hay and Artists of The Royal Ballet

©ROH/Johan Persson, 2014

TETRACTYS – THE ART OF FUGUE

Opposite page: Paul Kay, Steven McRae and Sarah Lamb

This page: Edward Watson, Natalia Osipova, Lauren Cuthbertson and Eric Underwood

©ROH/Johan Persson, 2014

GLORIA

This page:
Sarah Lamb and Thiago Soares

Opposite page:
Ryoichi Hirano and Artists of The Royal Ballet

©ROH/Johan Persson, 2014

THE SLEEPING BEAUTY

This page:

Top: Lauren Cuthbertson as Princess Aurora, Matthew Golding as Prince Florimund and Melissa Hamilton as the Lilac Fairy

Bottom: Akane Takada as Princess Aurora and Vadim Muntagirov as Prince Florimund

Opposite page: Marcelino Sambé as the Bluebird

©ROH/Tristram Kenton, 2014

THE WINTER'S TALE

This page: Edward Watson as Leontes, Lauren Cuthbertson as Hermione and Federico Bonelli as Polixenes

Opposite page: Sarah Lamb as Perdita and Steven McRae as Florizel

©ROH/Johan Persson, 2014

THE WINTER'S TALE

This page:

Top: Laura Morera as Paulina and Bennet Gartside as Antigonus

Bottom: Beatriz Stix-Brunell as Perdita and Vadim Muntagirov as Florizel, with Artists of The Royal Ballet

Opposite page:

Top: Artists of The Royal Ballet

Bottom: Marianela Nuñez as Hermione

©ROH/Johan Persson, 2014

SERENADE

This page: Marianela Nuñez and Artists of The Royal Ballet

Opposite page: Melissa Hamilton

©ROH/Tristram Kenton, 2014

SWEET VIOLETS

Opposite page:

Left: Thomas Whitehead as Robert Wood and Meaghan Grace Hinkis as Emily Dimmock

Right: Yuhui Choe as Little Dot

This page:

Top: Ryoichi Hirano as Robert Wood and Romany Pajdak as Emily Dimmock

Bottom: Alexander Campbell as Jack and Bennet Gartside as Walter Sickert

DGV: DANSE À GRANDE VITESSE

Opposite page: Zenaida Yanowsky and Eric Underwood

This page:

Top: Melissa Hamilton and Matthew Golding

Bottom: Artists of The Royal Ballet

©ROH/Tristram Kenton, 2014

THE DREAM

This page:
Paul Kay as Puck

Opposite page:
Matthew Golding as Oberon

©ROH/Bill Cooper, 2014

THE DREAM

Roberta Marquez as Titania, Bennet Gartside as Bottom and Steven McRae as Oberon

©ROH/Bill Cooper, 2014

CONNECTOME

Opposite page: Natalia Osipova and Artists of The Royal Ballet

This page: Steven McRae

THE CONCERT

This page:

Top: James Wilkie, Johannes Stepanek and Lauren Cuthbertson

Bottom: Artists of The Royal Ballet

Opposite page:

Top: Laura Morera and Bennet Gartside

Bottom: Robert Clark, Lauren Cuthbertson and Kristen McNally

DRAFT WORKS

Opposite page: Nicol Edmonds, Tristan Dyer and Tomas Mock in *Ingemisco*

This page:

Top: Isabella Gasparini, Kevin Emerton, Elsa Godard, Tomas Mock, Jacqueline Clark, Matthew Ball, Annette Buvoli and Reece Clarke in *Les deux, comme un*

Bottom:

Left: Tara-Brigitte Bhavnani and Romany Pajdak in *Untitled*

Right: Hayley Forskitt in *Matriarch*

P.10 **DON QUIXOTE**

Production and Choreography Carlos Acosta *after* Marius Petipa
Music Ludwig Minkus *arranged and orchestrated by* Martin Yates
Conductor Martin Yates

Designs Tim Hatley
Lighting design Hugh Vanstone
Ballet Master Christopher Saunders
Ballet Mistress Samantha Raine
Principal coaching Carlos Acosta, Alexander Agadzhanov, Lesley Collier, Jonathan Cope
Dance Notator Anna Trevien

Premiere

5 October 2013 (The Royal Ballet)

P.12 **ROMEO AND JULIET**

Choreography Kenneth MacMillan
Music Sergey Prokofiev
Conductor Barry Wordsworth

Designs Nicholas Georgiadis
Lighting design John B. Read
Staging Julie Lincoln, Christopher Saunders
Ballet Master Christopher Saunders
Ballet Mistress Samantha Raine
Principal coaching Alexander Agadzhanov, Lesley Collier, Jonathan Cope

Premiere

9 February 1965 (The Royal Ballet)

P.14 **CHROMA**

Choreography Wayne McGregor
Music Joby Talbot, Jack White III *arranged by* Joby Talbot *orchestrated by* Christopher Austin
Conductor Tom Seligman

Set designs John Pawson
Costume designs Moritz Junge
Lighting design Lucy Carter
Assistant to the Choreographer Antoine Vereecken
Ballet Master Gary Avis

Premiere

17 November 2006 (The Royal Ballet)

P.16 **THE HUMAN SEASONS**

Choreography David Dawson
Music Greg Haines
Conductor Barry Wordsworth

Set and projection design Eno Henze
Costume designs Yumiko Takeshima
Lighting design Bert Dalhuysen
Assistant to the Choreographer Tim Couchman
Dance Notator Amanda Eyles

Premiere

9 November 2013 (The Royal Ballet)

P.18 **THE RITE OF SPRING**

Choreography Kenneth MacMillan
Music Igor Stravinsky
Conductor Barry Wordsworth

Designs Sidney Nolan
Lighting design John B. Read
Staging Christopher Saunders
Ballet Master Christopher Saunders
Ballet Mistress Samantha Raine
Principal coaching Monica Mason

Premiere

3 May 1962 (The Royal Ballet)

P.20 **THE NUTCRACKER**

Choreography Peter Wright *after* Lev Ivanov
Music Pyotr Il'yich Tchaikovsky
Conductor Martin West
Original Scenario Marius Petipa *after* E.T.A. Hoffmann's Nussknacker und Mausekönig

Production and scenario Peter Wright
Designs Julia Trevelyan Oman
Lighting design Mark Henderson
Production Consultant Roland John Wiley
Staging Christopher Carr
Ballet Master Gary Avis
Ballet Mistress Samantha Raine
Principal coaching Alexander Agadzhanov, Gary Avis, Christopher Carr, Lesley Collier, Jonathan Cope, Christopher Saunders
Dance Notators Mayumi Hotta, Anna Trevien

Premiere

16 December 1892 (Mariinsky Theatre, St Petersburg)

20 December 1984 (The Royal Ballet, this production)

P.22 **JEWELS**

Choreography George Balanchine
Music Gabriel Fauré ('Emeralds')
Igor Stravinsky ('Rubies')
Pyotr Il'yich Tchaikovsky ('Diamonds')
Conductor Valery Ovsyanikov

Set designs Jean-Marc Puissant
Costume designs Barbara Karinska
Costume designs consultant Holly Hynes
Lighting Jennifer Tipton
Staging Elyse Borne, Patricia Neary
Ballet Master Christopher Saunders ('Rubies' and 'Diamonds')
Ballet Mistress Samantha Raine ('Emeralds')
Dance Notator Anna Trevien ('Diamonds')
Principal coaching Elyse Borne ('Emeralds' and 'Diamonds'), Patricia Neary ('Rubies'), Christopher Saunders ('Rubies' and 'Diamonds')

Premieres

13 April 1967 (New York City Ballet)

23 November 2007 (The Royal Ballet, this production)

P.24 **HANSEL AND GRETEL**

Choreography Liam Scarlett
Music Dan Jones

Designs Jon Bausor
Lighting design Paul Keogan

Premiere

8 May 2013 (The Royal Ballet)

P.26 **GISELLE**

Music Adolphe Adam *revised by* Joseph Horovitz
Choreography Marius Petipa *after* Jean Coralli *and* Jules Perrot
Scenario Théophile Gautier *after* Heinrich Heine
Conductor Boris Gruzin

Production and Additional Choreography Peter Wright
Designs John Macfarlane
Original lighting Jennifer Tipton *recreated by* David Finn
Staging Christopher Carr
Ballet Master Gary Avis
Ballet Mistress Samantha Raine
Principal coaching Alexander Agadzhanov, Lesley Collier, Jonathan Cope, Olga Evreinoff, Monica Mason, Peter Wright

Premieres

28 June 1841 (Paris: *Original choreography by* Jean Corelli and Jules Perrot; *Later versions by* Petipa, notably 1884)

1 January 1934 (Vic-Wells Ballet)

28 November 1985 (The Royal Ballet, this production)

P.28 **RHAPSODY**

Choreography Frederick Ashton
Music Sergey Rachmaninoff
Conductor Barry Wordsworth

Designs Jessica Curtis
Lighting design Neil Austin
Staging Christopher Carr, Grant Coyle
Principal coaching Alexander Agadzhanov, Lesley Collier
Dance Notator Grant Coyle

Premiere
4 August 1980
(The Royal Ballet)

P.30 **TETRACTYS – THE ART OF FUGUE**

Choreography Wayne McGregor
Music Johann Sebastian Bach
arranged and orchestrated by Michael Berkeley
Conductor Tim Murray

Set and costume designs Tauba Auerbach
Lighting design Lucy Carter
Ballet Master Gary Avis
Dance Notator Amanda Eyles

Premiere
7 February 2014
(The Royal Ballet)

P.32 **GLORIA**

Choreography Kenneth MacMillan
Music Francis Poulenc
Conductor Barry Wordsworth

Designs Andy Klunder
Lighting design John B. Read
Staging Christopher Saunders

Premiere
13 March 1980
(The Royal Ballet)

P.34 **THE SLEEPING BEAUTY**

Choreography Marius Petipa
Additional Choreography Frederick Ashton, Anthony Dowell, Christopher Wheeldon
Music Pyotr Il'yich Tchaikovsky
Conductor Valery Ovsyanikov

Production Monica Mason
and Christopher Newton
after Ninette de Valois
and Nicholas Sergeyev
Original designs Oliver Messel
Additional designs Peter Farmer
Lighting design Mark Jonathan
Staging Christopher Carr
Ballet Master Gary Avis
Ballet Mistress Samantha Raine
Principal coaching Alexander Agadzhanov, Lesley Collier, Jonathan Cope, Monica Mason
Dance Notator Grant Coyle

Premieres
20 February 1946
(Sadler's Wells Ballet)
15 May 2006
(The Royal Ballet, this production)

P.36 **THE WINTER'S TALE**

Choreography Christopher Wheeldon
Music Joby Talbot
Conductor David Briskin

Designs Bob Crowley
Lighting design Natasha Katz
Projection design Daniel Brodie
Silk effects design Basil Twist
Assistant to the Choreographer Jacquelin Barrett
Ballet Master Christopher Saunders
Assistant to the Ballet Master Jonathan Howells
Principal coaching Jonathan Cope
Dance Notator Anna Trevien

Premiere
10 April 2014
(The Royal Ballet)

P.40 **SERENADE**

Choreography George Balanchine
Music Pytor Il'yich Tchaikovsky
Conductor Pavel Sorokin

Costume designs Barbara Karinska
Staging Patricia Neary

Premieres
1 March 1935
(School of American Ballet)
7 May 1964
(The Royal Ballet)

P.42 **SWEET VIOLETS**

Choreography Liam Scarlett
Music Sergey Rachmaninoff

Designs John Macfarlane
Lighting design David Finn

Premiere
5 April 2012
(The Royal Ballet)

P.44 **DGV: DANSE À GRANDE VITESSE**

Choreography Christopher Wheeldon
Music Michael Nyman
Conductor Pavel Sorokin

Designs Jean-Marc Puissant
Lighting Jennifer Tipton
Staging Christopher Saunders

Premiere
17 November 2006
(The Royal Ballet)

P.46 **THE DREAM**

Choreography Frederick Ashton
Music Felix Mendelssohn
arranged by John Lanchbery
Conductor Barry Wordsworth

Designs David Walker
Lighting design John B. Read
Staging Anthony Dowell, Christopher Carr
Ballet Master Gary Avis
Principal coaching Lesley Collier, Anthony Dowell

Premiere
2 April 1964
(The Royal Ballet)

P.50 **CONNECTOME**

Choreography Alastair Marriott
Assistant to the Choreographer Jonathan Howells
Music Arvo Pärt
Conductor Barry Wordsworth

Set designs Es Devlin
Costume designs Jonathan Howells
Lighting design Bruno Poet
Video design Luke Halls

Premiere
31 May 2014
(The Royal Ballet)

P.52 **THE CONCERT**

Choreography Jerome Robbins
Music Fryderyk Chopin
arranged by Clare Grundman
Conductor Barry Wordsworth

Front cloth designs Saul Steinberg
Costume designs Irene Saraff
Original lighting Ronald Bates
Lighting Jennifer Tipton
Ballet Master Gary Avis

Premieres
6 March 1956
(New York City Ballet)
4 March 1975
(The Royal Ballet)

P.54 **DRAFT WORKS**

Choreography
Joshua Beamish (*L'inverno*)
Sander Blommaert (*Les deux, comme un*)
Kenta Kura (*DW2*)
Kristen McNally (*Matriarch*)
Erico Montes (*Prometheus*)
Aakash Odedra (*Untitled*)
Ludovic Ondiviela (*Untitled*)
Marcelino Sambé (*Preparations for the Last TV Fake*)
Valentino Zucchetti (*Ingemisco*)

Opposite page:
Clockwise from top left:

David Dawson in rehearsal for *The Human Seasons* with Marianela Nuñez

©ROH/Bill Cooper, 2013

Alastair Marriott in rehearsal for *Connectome* with Natalia Osipova

©ROH/Bill Cooper, 2014

Christopher Wheeldon in rehearsal for *The Winter's Tale* with Zenaida Yanowsky

©ROH/Johan Persson, 2014

Wayne McGregor in rehearsal for *Tetractys – The Art of Fugue* with Akane Takada and Federico Bonelli

©ROH/Johan Persson, 2014

SEASON REVIEW 2013/14

THE ROYAL BALLET TOUR TO MONACO AND TOKYO

A lot can happen in a Season – and for The Royal Ballet even between Seasons the activity hardly ever seems to stop. After the last performances of the 2012/13 Season at the Royal Opera House, The Royal Ballet left for Monaco for the start of their Summer tour: four performances of Kenneth MacMillan's *Manon* at the impressive Grimaldi Forum. It was quite a distance to the second part of the tour – Japan. But, even with such a dramatic change of culture and location, the reception was equally enthusiastic. The Company gave five sold-out performances of Artistic Associate Christopher Wheeldon's *Alice's Adventures in Wonderland* (its Asia premiere) and five more of Anthony Dowell's production of *Swan Lake* at the Bunka Kaikan, Tokyo's main concert hall.

The range of the Royal Ballet repertory and dancers was the defining feature of a gala performance on 10 July conducted by Boris Gruzin and Dominic Grier. The programme included the Bedroom *pas de deux* from MacMillan's *Manon* and an extract from the last act of his *Mayerling*, Frederick Ashton's Awakening *pas de deux* from *The Sleeping Beauty* and his *Voices Spring*, alongside the Act III *pas de deux* from *Don Quixote* and George Balanchine's *Symphony in C*. Contemporary pieces included McGregor's *Qualia pas de deux*, Wheeldon's *After the Rain*, Scarlett's *Jubilee pas de deux* and Marriott's *In the Hothouse*.

Once again The Royal Ballet tour delighted our international audiences, and a summer break was well deserved by all.

NEW WORKS AND CONTEMPORARY REVIVALS

The 2013/14 Season opened with energy and novelty in Carlos Acosta's exuberant and colourful new production of *Don Quixote*. With designs by Tim Hatley and a new arrangement and orchestration of Minkus's score by Martin Yates, the well-received production was a welcome addition to the Company's roster of full-length ballets. At the premiere Acosta danced the role of Basilio with Marianela Nuñez as Kitri. Christopher Saunders, William Tuckett and Gary Avis brought humour and gravity to the role of Don Quixote himself. *Don Quixote* was also broadcast into cinemas worldwide – the first ballet in the 2014/15 Royal Opera House Live Cinema Season, and it was released on DVD in April.

The Season also saw new work from David Dawson, Wayne McGregor, Christopher Wheeldon and Alastair Marriott.

The Human Seasons, Dawson's first work for the Company, had its world premiere in November 2014 in a mixed programme with McGregor's *Chroma* and MacMillan's *The Rite of Spring*. Inspired by John Keats's poem of the same name, Dawson's ballet combined his athletic and sculptural choreography with a new score from Greg Haines.

McGregor's *Tetractys – The Art of Fugue* received its premiere in February 2014, in a mixed programme with Ashton's *Rhapsody* and MacMillan's *Gloria*. *Tetractys* – set to extracts from Bach's contrapuntal masterpiece, orchestrated by Michael Berkeley, with abstract, geometrical designs by Tauba Auerbach – captured the fascinating mathematical complexity of Bach's music in choreography that echoes its range of shapes.

This page:
Tierney Heap and Ryoichi Hirano in Wheeldon's *DGV: Danse à grande vitesse*

©ROH/Tristram Kenton, 2014

Opposite page:
Top: Yuhui Choe and Kenta Kura in Mayuri Boonham's *The Human Edge*

©ROH/Andrej Uspenski, 2014

Bottom:
Melissa Hamilton and Eric Underwood in Alexander Whitley's *All that is Solid Melts into Air*

©ROH/Andrej Uspenski, 2014

Christopher Wheeldon created his second full-evening ballet for the Company, to follow his successful *Alice's Adventures in Wonderland* in 2011. His new adaptation of Shakespeare's *The Winter's Tale* was acclaimed, prompting Sarah Crompton in the *Telegraph* to write: '*The Winter's Tale* is a triumph. It is contemporary and classical, traditional and modern, narrative and abstract. It feels like something entirely new'.

Alastair Marriott completed the offering of new work with *Connectome*, his first choreography for the main stage since 2012's 'Trespass' (*Metamorphosis: Titian 2012*, created in collaboration with Wheeldon). The ballet was inspired by scientific research into the possible identification of a person's memories, personality and intellect with the connections between brain cells. New young casts were given the chance to shine alongside two Principal casts: Osipova, Watson and McRae; and Lamb, Cervera and Campbell.

Liam Scarlett's *Hansel and Gretel*, which received its premiere in the 2012/13 Season, was given its first revival with many dancers from its original casts, and the addition of Luca Acri as Hansel (alongside James Hay). Donald Thom and Ryoichi Hirano, stood out again in the eerie, complex roles of the Sandman and the Witch. Scarlett's *Sweet Violets* – his atmospheric interpretation of the art of Walter Sickert and the violent London underworld of the early 20th century – was also revived with new casts.

Other contemporary revivals included McGregor's *Chroma* and Wheeldon's *DGV: Danse à grande vitesse*, with debuts for Olivia Cowley and Beatriz Stix-Brunell in *Chroma* and new casts for *DGV* including Tierney Heap and Akane Takada.

THE ROYAL BALLET STUDIO PROGRAMME

New works by Alexander Whitley and Mayuri Boonham were created as part of The Royal Ballet Studio Programme in the Linbury Studio Theatre. Boonham and Whitley were Choreographic Affiliates of the Studio Programme and these new works were the result.

The Studio Programme also saw the revival of Arthur Pita's dance theatre adaptation of Kafka's *The Metamorphosis*, and visiting companies including Ballet Black (their 13th year in the Linbury), Northern Ballet, Phoenix Dance Theatre, National Dance Company Wales, De Oscuro Dance and Company Chameleon. The Linbury once again hosted the London International Mime Festival. HeadSpaceDance also returned with a mixed programme, and 'Springboard' – The Royal Ballet's showcase for burgeoning junior companies – brought performances from Ballet Central, Dutch National Juniors (under the creative tutelage of former Royal Ballet dancer Ernest Meisner), Rambert and Verve, the performing company of Northern School of Contemporary Dance.

Draft Works – The Royal Ballet's annual platform for Company dancers and invited guests to experiment with choreographic sketches – returned with nine new pieces of choreography from Royal Ballet dancers Sander Blommaert, Kenta Kura, Kristen McNally, Eric Montes, Ludovic Ondiviela, Marcelino Sambé and Valentino Zucchetti, and visiting choreographers Joshua Beamish and Aakash Odedra. Odedra's Draft Work was the first draft of his piece for Deloitte Ignite 14.

COMPANY CLASSICS AND MINIATURE GEMS

The classics were not in short supply in the 2013/14 Season. Peter Wright's timeless *Giselle*, always an audience favourite, returned to the stage with two new Giselles, Laura Morera and Natalia Osipova; Osipova's debut was broadcast live in cinemas in January 2014. There were popular Christmas performances of *The Nutcracker* and well-received February performances of *The Sleeping Beauty*, in which Yuhui Choe made her debut as Princess Aurora and Ryoichi Hirano his as Prince Florimund.

MacMillan's *Romeo and Juliet*, *The Rite of Spring* (with an impressive debut by Claudia Dean in the role of The Chosen Maiden) and *Gloria* (with Melissa Hamilton making her debut), were also revived.

Performances of Ashton's glorious adaptation from Shakespeare, *The Dream*, marked 50 years since the ballet was created on the Company. Anthony Dowell and Antoinette Sibley – the couple on whom the roles of Oberon and Titania were created in 1964 – coached the Principal roles and shared the curtain call with the opening night's cast on the Royal Opera House stage. The return of Ashton's *Rhapsody* saw debuts from Yuhui Choe, Valentino Zucchetti, Francesca Hayward and James Hay.

Balanchine's *Serenade*, performed in May (with *Sweet Violets* and *DGV*) brought opportunities for several debuts including Natalia Osipova, Olivia Cowley, Melissa Hamilton and Matthew Golding, and Balanchine's *Jewels* once again showed off the sparkling precision, grace and humour of Principals, Soloists and corps de ballet.

The Dream appeared in the last mixed programme of the Season with *Connectome* and Jerome Robbins's highly entertaining *The Concert* – a joyous and welcome return to the repertory after 13 years. *The Concert* brought Royal Ballet Head of Music Staff Robert Clark to the stage as the Pianist, and some witty and raucous entertainment from all ranks of the Company.

This page: Valentino Zucchetti as Puck in Ashton's *The Dream*

©ROH/Bill Cooper, 2014

Opposite page: Zenaida Yanowsky as The Chosen Maiden in MacMillan's *The Rite of Spring*

©ROH/Bill Cooper, 2013

At the end of the Season the Company left for Moscow, Taipei and Shanghai.

There was much activity outside the Royal Opera House during the 2013/14 Season too. In November 2013, Guest Principal Character Artist Will Tuckett created a new ballet to music by Martin Yates, *Elizabeth*, which was performed in the Painted Hall at the Old Royal Naval College in Greenwich. Royal Ballet Principals Zenaida Yanowsky and Carlos Acosta danced with Laura Caldow, and actress Lindsay Duncan performed words written by Alastair Middleton. In June, Yanowsky performed another Tuckett work, which he created on her for Tate Modern's live cinema broadcast accompanying their sold-out exhibition 'Matisse: The Cut-Outs'.

Principals Marianela Nuñez and Thiago Soares, as well as Soloist Fernando Montaño were all nominated in the LUKAS awards in May, celebrating the culture of Latin American, Spanish and Portuguese communities in the UK. Montaño won the Latin Personality of the Year Award for a second year.

Following the success of Andrej Uspenski's first photography book, *Dancers*, Oberon Books published a collection of Andrej's images of Principal Steven McRae – *Steven McRae: Dancer in the Fast Lane* – in July.

At the annual National Dance Awards presented by the the Critics' Circle, in January 2014, former Principal Leanne Benjamin was presented with the Critics' Circle De Valois Award for outstanding achievement. Artistic Associate Christopher Wheeldon won the award for Best Classical Choreography for the previous Season's *Aeternum*, and Principal Natalia Osipova was also honoured for her performances with the Mikhailovsky Ballet, Bolshoi Ballet and The Royal Ballet.

BALLET HEALTHCARE BY NICHOLAS MANDERSON

This page: The Royal Ballet's Mason Healthcare Suite at the Royal Opera House with, from left, Clinical Director Greg Retter, Gyrotonic and Pilates Instructor Fiona Kleckham, Sports Scientist Patrick Rump, Head of Physiotherapy Services Moira McCormack, Healthcare Team Assistant Olivia Powell, Soft Tissue Therapist Konrad Simpson, Body Control Instructor Jane Paris and Senior Physiotherapist Aedin Kennedy.

©ROH/Sim Cannety-Clarke, 2014

It's no mean feat for The Royal Ballet to deliver the performances we all enjoy on stage with such perfection, intensity of emotion and artistic beauty. When we think of ballet we most likely think of a traditional art form handed down through generations of dancers and choreographers for centuries, or the contemporary, sometimes more abstract, movement that has that tradition as its foundation.

But at the heart of all performance, from the most traditional to the most abstract, is the physicality of the art form itself, the athletic bodies in motion.

Around the core of the traditional daily ballet class, the Company has a host of professionals and disciplines to support the dancers, and continually embraces new methods and techniques to enable the dancers to achieve their peak. 'The important thing is the final objective', says Principal Federico Bonelli, 'and for us it is the performance.' While we are used to the concept of sports sciences and medicine in relation to athletes, surprisingly we seem to expect it less when it comes to ballet, the most athletic of art forms.

The Royal Ballet's Mason Healthcare Suite, which opened at the Royal Opera House at the start of the 2013/14 Season, brings together the professions that maintain and improve the quality of the Company's dance and performance. Clinical Director for Ballet Healthcare, Greg Retter, previously managed the Intensive Rehabilitation Unit for the British Olympic Association before joining the Company in 2013. Greg notes that in the healthcare suite 'there isn't any discipline or equipment you wouldn't find being used by top Olympic athletes or at a Premiership football club'.

The Mason Healthcare Suite provides a comprehensive system of physiotherapy, Pilates, sports science, medicine, psychology, podiatry, nutrition, osteopathy and soft tissue therapy. The healthcare team are able to provide each dancer with a bespoke plan of practices and treatments to suit their individual needs. At the core of this work is pre-habilitation, which Greg Retter describes as 'a proactive approach to developing a stronger more robust dancer who is better equipped to withstand the rigours of a classical ballet workload – after all, why wait until someone suffers an injury to address a problem?'. Every dancer is comprehensively screened at the beginning of each Season. This not only provides the healthcare professionals with useful information about each dancer's overall fitness and wellbeing but also highlights any potential weaknesses, which they can then address directly.

Brian Maloney, a former Royal Ballet Soloist, is now part of the Sports Science team, and specializes in strength and conditioning. Brian also takes the morning ballet class three times a week. 'I love the synchronicity between class and the artists' gym work', he explains. The crossover enables him to see 'how they are dancing, where the technical faults might be and where we can work to develop and further change both disciplines.'

Preparation of the muscles, tendons, ligaments, bones and tissue for the impacts of performance and training can be simulated with carefully designed weights exercises: 'When you're doing a full jump in ballet you're transferring more than six times your weight through your body. How can you replicate that in a safe manner? Well, through an incremental process, you can load someone up with weights, in a controlled environment, which is generally safer

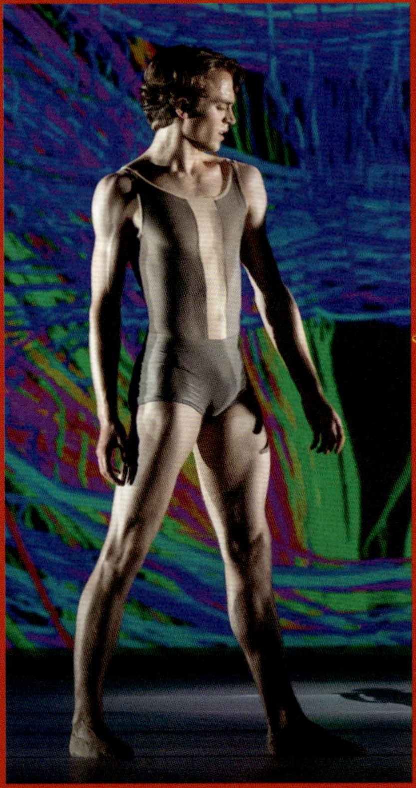

Artist Matthew Ball joined The Royal Ballet from The Royal Ballet School in the 2013/14 Season. However, his entry into the Company was delayed due to necessary surgery on his knee. He talks about identifying that something was wrong, the treatment and support he received and the contrasts between life at the School and life as an Artist with the Company.

'I had experienced some problems and pains with my left knee, before I joined the Company. I went to see Moira McCormack (Head of Physiotherapy) who referred me to a specialist and had some MRI scans. It turned out I had some damage to my knee. A segment of bone and cartilage had started to come loose, which required an operation. The segment was secured with three long, plastic screws that eventually dissolved, and I wasn't to bend my knee for the following six weeks.

That was in April 2013, so when the 2013/14 Season began I was only just returning to taking ballet classes. It was "baby steps", taking it easy and gradually building up strength. The first time you return to doing something it can be quite intimidating but you take it in your stride, and do it carefully.

Not having had an injury before and being new to the Company, I hadn't experienced the close attention and bespoke programmes that the healthcare department develop for you. I hadn't expected that using heavy weights would be part of a ballet recovery programme and that it would support and improve my ballet, but I enjoyed both the strength and conditioning training. You realize it helps take the pressure off the joint and put the load and force through the muscle, reducing the overall strain. As a result I feel much more confident now than I did before my injury. The chance to speak to a sports psychologist was also a very valuable experience. It helped me to develop ways to deal with mental blocks, negativity and, more importantly, ways to improve my focus.'

Matthew appeared in Alastair Marriott's *Connectome* in June.

than putting the body through strain that it isn't ready for. If you can better prepare for such forces going through your body, you reduce the risk of injury.' Ultimately for Brian, and the healthcare team as a whole, it's about getting the best of both worlds: helping to 'develop a healthier, happier dancer; gaining all the benefits'.

The process of pre-habilitation adds a level of security to ballet practice. Dancers can improve their overall wellbeing and fitness without adding to the existing rigours of rehearsal and performance through the support and development available in the controlled environment of the healthcare suite.

This is something Federico Bonelli has utilized in his approach to training and rehearsal. Traditionally, dancers have trained by repetition, practising in the studio the movements they do on stage until they develop the stamina to be able to do them well. But such repetition takes its toll on the body. 'Every time I jump or lift somebody there is a certain amount of stress on the joints, the bones, the tendons. The idea behind the gym and healthcare suite is to develop the strength but take out of the equation some of the stress. You can't eliminate stress completely but when you go into the rehearsal studio, which can never be replaced, and practice the coordination or take class (which I do almost everyday) the idea is that you become so well prepared you can do it all better right away; instead of having to repeat it over and over again. Too much repetition and strain is what exposes you to injury.'

While there is a definite security for the dancer in rehearsing by repetition, it is not necessarily the most productive use of rehearsal time. So separate conditioning and strength training gives them the opportunity to focus on technique when in the studio. 'In *The Sleeping Beauty*', Federico recalls, 'there are four double *Tours en L'air* in the Act III solo. I would maybe twenty or twenty-five in the rehearsal. But that's not always possible with a full rehearsal schedule. So you have to rehearse more intelligently – you don't spend an hour of rehearsal doing a ten-minute section of the ballet, you can go through a whole act of the ballet in that hour.' This is a helpful efficiency, given the broad range of repertory the dancers rehearse simultaneously: 'the next hour you have to switch back and do something else – and there are only a certain number of jumps that I am able to do in a day before my body becomes fatigued.' The same is true of the strength conditioning, which can itself take its toll on the body, and so must be practised at times to maximize its benefit – such as at the end of the day when there is no performance – 'I would never do weights before a performance!'.

The recovery process after rehearsal is also carefully managed. 'At the end of my working day I might go and see the massuers/soft tissue specialists to increase the circulation so that I can recover faster during the night. I'll visit the Physiotherapists if I have a problem.' Rest time and diet are also crucial: 'I find myself thinking a lot about finding time to eat and getting enough food and fluid into my system to be able to keep going. You have to put the fuel into your body.'

Opposite page:
Matthew Ball in Alastair Marriott's *Connectome*

This page:
Federico Bonelli Act III solo from *The Sleeping Beauty*

Fiona Kleckham, Body Control Instructor

Fiona has been at the Royal Opera House since 2006. She trained in ballet and contemporary dance at Laban Centre London and after dancing and teaching in Hong Kong, she retrained as a Pilates teacher, qualifying in 1998. With further training in Florence and Rome she gained qualifications from the Gyrotonic Foundation and now specializes in teaching Gyrotonic in a dance environment for The Royal Ballet.

'Gyrotonic is a movement system separate from Pilates and still lesser known as a way of supporting and enhancing the work of a dancer. In Italy, for example, where I did most of my training, it's probably more popular than Pilates, but it's gaining recognition here and is popular with dancers of all levels in the Company.

The system, which is over thirty years old, started with floor work, now known as Gyrokinesis, and progressed to include work with machines. The main piece of specifically designed apparatus here is the Gyrotonic Pulley Tower. On it I work one-to-one with the dancer, for just 30 minutes, an hour or longer, depending on their schedule, either focusing on a particular issue or a general workout.

Gyrotonic is a very three-dimensional movement system, based on spiralling and circular movements with a focus on both strength and flexibility. It increases endurance, the range of motion and improves coordination. But it is also about creating space in your joints, ligaments, in your skeleton and also in your head! It helps create an awareness of the body and space and moving with ease, which translates very well into dance. You take that with you into class, rehearsal and performance.

The movement sequences have specific breathing patterns too – which can be quite challenging for dancers not used to showing that they are breathing! – similar to breathing in yoga, there are kinds and patterns of inhaling and exhaling.

Gyrotonic is very much about coordination and patterns – you aren't just working one body part, it's the whole body working all the time. Its an awakening and a workout for the whole body.

A healthy body helps create a healthy mind, and the fitter the individual, the better their performance can be. Hopefully pain and injury and time away from dance can be kept to an absolute minimum.'

Principal Lauren Cuthbertson agrees that pre-habilitation is key to the confidence she has on stage: 'The fitter you are, the more protected you are, and you can really go for it in the studio or on stage.' For her, the confidence inspired by conditioning and fitness allows for more creative freedom of expression: 'You can concentrate on the ballet rather than worrying about stamina and strength. For me it's a massive assistance to what I want to do and create. There's not a day that I won't do something from part of one of my programmes to keep moving on. I have a personal routine that I have developed over the years with various people, with different specialities in the healthcare team. It's a long-term programme of things that I work on with specific goals – certain weaknesses and prevention – and short term goals for specific roles that might require a bit more stamina or particular movements, like a lift with a partner that isn't quite right yet.'

Unfortunately injury does feature in the life of professional ballet dancers. But the healthcare suite and team aid and support the dancers throughout their treatment, full recovery and rehabilitation. And the support doesn't stop once they have returned to the stage.

After injury, Lauren explains, the Company healthcare support is 'a place of refuge where I've been able to start from scratch and build up again. Though the healthcare suite is a relatively small space within the Royal Opera House it's a whole world of organization, dedication and so much emotion. Everyone is going through something different or they are at different stages of their rehabilitation'.

The emotional impact of injury and rehabilitation, too, is something the Company takes seriously. 'It's one of the worst times professionally for a dancer', says Lauren, and without the provision of a dedicated and understanding group of support staff the experience can be isolating.

'I've developed a really close relationship with Jane Paris (Body Control Instructor), who has helped me through both of my main rehabilitations, from after surgery to returning to the stage. I've been working with Jane since my second Season with the Company and still now it's like she has a Mary Poppins bag of exercises! You go to her with some concern and she brings out something completely new, but still using the same equipment that we've been using for ages. It's an evolving world and it can be adapted to anything you need.'

As technology evolves, so the treatment methods that support ballet conditioning and performance must keep up. Some of the equipment may be quite specialist but it all works to assist in and to simulate the stresses and movements of ballet: 'It re-creates what we do as dancers', explains Lauren, 'it really gives you the confidence in yourself and your body when you're rehabilitating or working on prevention. Your body is the tool you work with daily and you will work with it until you retire. We have to get the best we can out of it, and as much as we can.'

The strength of the Royal Ballet healthcare provision lies in this interdisciplinary approach – it is the sum of the whole team working around the dancers to support them in their careers.

Konrad Simpson, Soft Tissue Therapist

Konrad joined the Company in 2007 as a Soft Tissue Therapist. His background is in dance: having graduated from Central School of Ballet in 1992, he was a dancer with Northern Ballet and San Francisco Ballet for eight years. Konrad retrained at the London School of Massage and London School of Sports Massage, graduating in 2001. Sports Massage is a combination of massage techniques that help prevent injury, improve the recovery time of muscles and generally relax the dancer's body and increase their range of motion and flexibility to let them perform at their best.

'I use a whole range of techniques to treat each individual dancer. Deep tissue work really gets stuck in; it can get muscle to release but it can be quite painful too. Compression generally gets the blood flowing. Swedish massage is a good starting point leading on to other treatments. Trigger therapy targets areas that are painful to the touch, where there might be slight tissue damage. Stretching too forms an important role.

Ballet is very repetitive and a dancer may spend a long time repeating the same movements. A choreographer or répétiteur will say 'let's see that again' and the dancer will repeat a movement maybe six or seven times. Using the same muscle groups so many times the muscle becomes overloaded. Massage identifies that and pounds it out, so the muscle releases and the next day they can carry on; rather than that tension building up to the point where it becomes a problem.

The dancers here are very lucky: not many companies have these facilities. The healthcare suite has everything the dancers might need and it's there to allow them to be their best. When I started as a dancer, we didn't have a physio or massage – if you were injured you went to an external physio and it would be a different one each time. Each physio would have their own approach so there was very little consistency. Here, the more you treat the dancers, the more you understand the way their body is and the way it responds to treatments. When you treat someone over a long period you get to understand how they react to what you're doing and what works.'

Fiona Kleckham and Konrad Simpson headshots

©ROH/Rob Moore, 2013

Lauren Cuthbertson and Edward Watson in rehearsal for Wheeldon's *The Winter's Tale*

©ROH/Johan Persson, 2014

BEHIND THE PROSCENIUM: BALLET STAGE MANAGEMENT BY GERARD DAVIS

'This is a Main House call. Ladies and gentlemen of The Royal Ballet, this is your half-hour call for this evening's performance of *Swan Lake*. You have thirty minutes. The red light is off, the stage is now available.'

A call like this is broadcast around the backstage areas of the Royal Opera House half an hour before every show. It's the first signal that things are almost ready for the performance and dancers in full costume begin to gather on stage. Around them the various technical crews are ready, having ensured that scenery, props and lighting are all in place, while the Front of House team begin to usher the audience into the auditorium in anticipation of lights down. At the centre of it all is the Stage Manager: the show won't go on until they give the word.

To arrive at 'the half' for an opening performance takes months of preparation. Johanna Adams Farley is The Royal Ballet's Senior Stage Manager. She has been with the Company since 1995, having worked at London Festival Ballet and Berlin's Deutsche Oper, and heads a team of three that includes Sarah Woodward (Deputy Stage Manager) and Alice Horsey (Assistant Stage Manager). Well before any ballet reaches the stage, the three liaise with departments across the Royal Opera House including the ballet Company and the Music, Wardrobe, Shoes, Press, Props, Production, Technical and Sound departments. They produce vital paperwork (such as risk assessments and essential technical plots) for each production and, among many other things, they are also responsible for more esoteric tasks such as hiring pianos for main stage performances and ensuring that actors and actresses are recruited and paid. 'Almost everything that ends up on the stage comes through us', says Johanna. 'With opera Stage Management, which is a different animal, staff are assigned to specific productions, but in ballet Stage Management, the three of us work on every performance of every ballet.'

The ability to read music is a prerequisite for the job as all the factors needed to run a successful live show are marked in a specially prepared musical score known as the prompt book. Every Royal Ballet production has its own prompt book, some date back decades, and for a new production this has to be created from scratch. Depending on the choreographer or scale of the ballet, one of the team (determined by Johanna at the start of the Season) will be present at different stages of the creative process.

Johanna explains: 'For one of Wayne McGregor's one-act abstract ballets like *Qualia* or *Tetractys – The Art of Fugue*, our involvement starts quite late in the rehearsal process, usually when we're approaching the first technical and lighting rehearsal. However, a longer work like *Raven Girl* – and I imagine the new *Woolf Works* ballet will be the same – one or all of us will be in from the beginning, depending on the props required and the different aspects of the set he wants to use. For Christopher Wheeldon's full-length *The Winter's Tale*, which had its premiere last Season, the set was so crucial we were all basically in the studio with the models and plans for every single rehearsal.'

Opposite page: Prompt corner as seen from backstage

This page: The view from prompt corner: Federico Bonelli in Balanchine's *Apollo*

his page:
arah Lamb
n Wheeldon's
lectric
ounterpoint
©ROH/Johan
ersson, 2010

pposite page:
eft: Beatriz
tix-Brunell as
lice in *Alice's*
dventures in
Wonderland
©ROH/Bill
ooper, 2012

ight: The Royal
allet Stage
Management
eam: Johanna
dams Farley
centre) with
lice Horsey
left) and Sarah
Woodward
right).
©ROH/Andrej
Jspenski, 2014

Tucked away to the front of stage-right is a space known as prompt corner which, during a show, is ablaze with an array of switches, flashing lights and TV monitors. It also has a great view across the stage. 'This is the hub of all main stage performances', explains Lynne Otto. Lynne retired from the Company at the start of the 2013/14 Season after 18 years as Deputy Stage Manager and now works freelance. From this nerve centre, whichever member of the Stage Management team is in charge of prompt corner can communicate directly with the Lighting Board Operator, the Fly Floor, Electrics and Back and Front of House (it's the Stage Manager, for instance, who announces that the audience must take their seats before the show starts, and the Front of House Manager needs to let Stage Management know if there are hold-ups with the audience). There is a TV monitor showing the full stage from the back of the auditorium; there's one fixed on the conductor and an infra-red screen that reveals what's happening when the stage is in darkness. Furthermore the other two members of Stage Management will be working around the stage to coordinate things and help ensure everything's running smoothly.

Opposite page:
Artists of The Royal Ballet in Ashton's *Les Patineurs*

During the performance, a vital part of Stage Management's responsibility is cueing. Stage Management doesn't cue every dancer onto the stage (it is part of the dancing so the dancers cue themselves) but they must make sure that elements such as scenery, special effects (gunshots or smoke for example) and lighting changes all happen safely and at the right time. Backstage it is not uncommon to hear arresting announcements from prompt corner such as, 'Stand by for the raising and lowering of Fritz' (when in *The Nutcracker* Drosselmeyer's magic enchants young Fritz so that he 'flies' above the stage). Often a complex series of cues is required – 'Electrics, lightning and pyrotechnics, and to start the smoke in the carriage, stand by for the exit of Carabosse' – to achieve some of the most memorable of ballet moments. There are so many things that go on behind the scenes – Stage Management doesn't pause for one moment during the whole performance.

Stage Management is the show's bridge between its technical and artistic aspects. 'In *Alice's Adventures in Wonderland*, for example, the way the tiny door interacts with Alice is all choreographed by Christopher Wheeldon', explains Lynne, 'but it's physically controlled by one of the Electrics crew. However, it's up to the person in prompt corner to guide them verbally by following the cues in their musical score. There are often animated objects in our shows – it almost makes us an extra dancer!'

In fact, it's often Wheeldon's ballets that Lynne has found to be the most technically complex. For *Electric Counterpoint*, Wheeldon's 2008 ballet in which live dancers interact with recorded video projections of themselves, 'we had to open and close doors precisely in time with the music. That was tricky. But the great thing about Christopher is that he's very organized, and once he's decided on his vision he's very good at conveying it to the other departments and doesn't often change his mind. Also, the first act of *Alice's Adventures* was originally 70 minutes long, and with all those different scenes the concentration involved was quite challenging. But by the first night everyone knew exactly what they were doing and it was a pleasure.'

With such planning and concentration on the detail, surprises are rare. But with live theatre very occasionally something doesn't go exactly according to plan. Once, during a Royal Ballet performance on tour in Frankfurt, the local curtain operator accidentally took the curtain out too early on *The Sleeping Beauty*, catching the stage team still setting the scenery. More recently at Covent Garden during an open General Rehearsal of *Les Patineurs* the snow that is supposed to fall gently towards the end of the ballet all came down in one go, to the surprise of the dancers and to the delight of the audience. The theatrical effect was of course still magical.

For Lynne, the show is very much focused on the dancers. 'We're their little support car driving along behind them helping them with whatever they need – our role is just to try to take as much stress out of the situation as possible so they can concentrate on the dancing. That's the best part of the job for me: it's a joy to go to work and watch world-class ballet dancers performing.'

There's a tremendous energy on the Royal Opera House stage, the choreographers, dancers, designers and technicians all work in an artform they love, with a heritage to be proud of. 'It's a sort of nervous energy', explains Johanna, 'I always feel it with *The Sleeping Beauty*, particularly when it comes to the boat journey. That music! It's always been special in the various productions I've been involved with. *Beauty* is one of my favourite ballets, because of its history with The Royal Ballet, and because of the performances I've seen and been a part of over the years. I saw Fonteyn dance Aurora, and that, for me, was one of the great experiences.'

A final message is broadcast to backstage: 'This is a Main House call, ladies and gentlemen, five minutes until curtain down on *Swan Lake*. Five minutes, thank you.'

Five minutes later, the curtain falls. The dancers take their bows and curtain calls and the auditorium gradually empties. When the dancers have left the stage, the stage crew strike the scenery and props. After a long, hard day the Stage Management team thank all the technical crews, and Johanna, after first going back to her office to write a detailed show report, can finally head for home, satisfied with another successful performance.

A COMPANY CHRONOLOGY

1930s

1931 20 January Bizet's opera *Carmen* is staged at the newly reopened Sadler's Wells Theatre. The dancers in it come from a fledgling ballet company, the Vic-Wells Opera Ballet, under the creative direction of their founder Ninette de Valois. The result of many developments of this Company – always under De Valois' leadership – would eventually be The Royal Ballet. **5 May** The Company gives its own performance of short works by De Valois at Lilian Baylis's Old Vic theatre. It is Baylis's use of dancers in her operas and plays that gives De Valois the chance to bring her Company together. **July** The Camargo Society presents the Company in a programme that includes De Valois' *Job* and two works by Frederick Ashton, a young dancer also beginning to make his mark as a choreographer.

1932 January Alicia Markova becomes a regular Guest Artist alongside Anton Dolin. **March** *Les Sylphides* is revived with Markova and Dolin. **September** The Company tours for the first time together, to Denmark. **October** Act II of *Le Lac des cygnes* marks the Company's first foray into the classical repertory.

1933 March Nicholas Sergeyev presents the full-length *Coppélia* with Lydia Lopokova as Swanilda. He had been the *régisseur general* of the Mariinsky Theatre, but fled Russia after the October Revolution, bringing the written notation necessary to classic Russian ballets.

1934 January Sergeyev puts on *Giselle* with Markova and Dolin. **April** *Casse-Noisette* is presented, again by Sergeyev. **20 November** The full *Le Lac des cygnes* is presented with Markova and Robert Helpmann, who had recently been promoted to Principal with the Company.

1935 Ashton is signed up as a performer and Resident Choreographer. **20 May** De Valois' *The Rake's Progress* has its first performance, with Markova as the Betrayed Girl. **26 November** Ashton's *Le Baiser de la fée* receives its premiere, with the young Margot Fonteyn in the cast.

1937 The Company represents British culture at the International Exhibition in Paris. **16 February** The premiere of Ashton's *Les Patineurs*. **27 April** A further Ashton premiere with *A Wedding Bouquet*. **5 October** De Valois' *Checkmate* receives its first performance in London. **25 November** Lilian Baylis dies.

1939 2 February Sergeyev puts on *The Sleeping Princess* with Fonteyn and Helpmann in the lead roles. **1 September** Germany invades Poland; in response, Britain, France, Australia and New Zealand declare war on Germany.

1940s

1940 23 January The first performance of Ashton's *Dante Sonata*. **May** The Company travels to the Netherlands for a small tour, but the advancing German army forces a hurried escape. **November** The Company begins to tour throughout Britain during wartime.

1941 The New Theatre, St Martin's Lane, becomes the Company's home for much of the war, and *The Sleeping Princess* is again staged.

1942 **19 May** The first performance of Helpmann's ballet *Hamlet*, with Helpmann in the title role.

1944 **26 October** Helpmann's *Miracle in the Gorbals* receives its premiere.

1945 The Company undertakes a tour of the Continent with the Entertainments National Service Association (ENSA), a forces organization. **May 8th** The war ends in Europe.

1946 **20 February** The Company becomes resident at Covent Garden, and reopens the Royal Opera House with *The Sleeping Beauty*. **24 April** Ashton's *Symphonic Variations* is performed for the first time.

1947 **February** De Valois invites Léonide Massine, one of the biggest stars of Diaghilev's Ballets Russes, to revive *The Three-Cornered Hat* and *La Boutique fantasque*.

1948 **23 December** Ashton's *Cinderella* receives its premiere: it is the Company's first home-grown full-length ballet.

1949 **9 October** The Company presents *The Sleeping Beauty* in New York, the start of a hugely successful tour that takes in many cities in the USA and Canada.

1950s

1950 **20 February** The first performance of De Valois' *Don Quixote*. **5 April** George Balanchine and his New York City Ballet make their first European visit, Balanchine reviving his *Ballet Imperial* for Sadler's Wells Ballet. **5 May** Roland Petit's creation for the Company, *Ballabile*, receives its premiere. **September** The Company embarks on a five-month, 32-city tour of the USA.

1951 **21 August** Music Director Constant Lambert, one of the chief architects of the Company with De Valois and Ashton, dies aged 45.

1952 **3 September** The first performance of Ashton's *Sylvia*.

1953 **2 June** Coronation gala for HM The Queen, which includes a specially devised ballet by Ashton for the occasion, *Homage to the Queen*.

1954 **23 August** For the 25th anniversary of Diaghilev's death, the Company joins the Edinburgh Festival tributes with a performance of *The Firebird*; Fonteyn dances the title role.

1956 **1 March** Kenneth MacMillan creates his first ballet for the Sadler's Wells Ballet, *Noctambules*. **31 October** The Sadler's Wells Ballet, the Sadler's Wells Theatre Ballet and the School are granted a Royal Charter – the main Company becoming The Royal Ballet.

1957 **1 January** John Cranko's *The Prince of the Pagodas*, to a new score by Benjamin Britten, is given its first performance at Covent Garden. It is the first full-length work to a modern commissioned score to be presented in the West.

1958 **27 October** Ashton's new ballet *Ondine*, created for Fonteyn, opens with her in the title role; the new score is by Hans Werner Henze.

1959 **13 March** MacMillan's *Danses concertantes*, created for Sadler's Wells Theatre Ballet in 1955, opens at Covent Garden.

1960s

1960 **28 January** The premiere of Ashton's 'tribute to nature', *La Fille mal gardée* with Nadia Nerina dancing the role of Lise to David Blair's Colas.

1961 **15 June** The Company makes its first tour of Russia presenting *Ondine* on the first night; an exchange agreement sees the Kirov Ballet perform at Covent Garden.

1962 **21 February** Rudolf Nureyev, having controversially defected from the Kirov in 1961, makes his debut as Albrecht to Fonteyn's Giselle. **3 May** MacMillan's new version of *The Rite of Spring*, with Monica Mason as The Chosen Maiden, is given its first performance.

1963 **12 March** Ashton's *Marguerite and Armand*, created for Fonteyn and Nureyev, opens. **7 May** De Valois retires as Director of the Company and Ashton succeeds her, while De Valois becomes supervisor of The Royal Ballet School. **28 November** Nureyev's first staging for The Royal Ballet is the 'Kingdom of the Shades' scene from *La Bayadère*.

Opposite page: Frederick Ashton rehearses Margot Fonteyn and members of the Sadler's Wells Ballet for a revival of *Symphonic Variations* (1946)

Photograph by Roger Wood ©ROH Collections

This page: Stanley Holden as Widow Simone and Leslie Edwards as Farmer Thomas in Ashton's *La Fille mal gardée*, 1960

©Houston Rogers/V&A Images

Antoinette Sibley as Manon and Anthony Dowell as Des Grieux in MacMillan's *Manon*, 1974

©Leslie E. Spatt

1964 29 February Antoinette Sibley dances Princess Aurora in the Company's 400th performance of *The Sleeping Beauty*. **2 April** The Company's contributions to the celebrations of the 400th anniversary of Shakespeare's birth include Ashton's *The Dream*, which launches the dance partnership of Sibley and Anthony Dowell. **2 December** Bronislava Nijinska, younger sister of Nijinsky, revives her *Les Biches*, with Svetlana Beriosova as the Hostess.

1965 9 February MacMillan's first full-length work, *Romeo and Juliet*, is presented; created for Lynn Seymour and Christopher Gable, the opening night is danced by Fonteyn and Nureyev.

1966 23 March Nijinska revives her *Les Noces* in a double bill with *Les Biches*. **May** MacMillan takes up the ballet directorship of the Deutsche Oper Berlin. **19 May** MacMillan's *Song of the Earth*, created for Cranko's Stuttgart Ballet, is given its Covent Garden premiere.

1967 25 January Antony Tudor creates his first work for The Royal Ballet, *Shadowplay*.

1968 29 February The premiere of Nureyev's version of *The Nutcracker*. **26 April** The Company makes the official announcement of Ashton's retirement as Director in 1970 and his succession by MacMillan. **25 October** The premiere of Ashton's *Enigma Variations*. **12 November** Tudor revives his 1938 production of *Lilac Garden*.

1970s

1971 22 July MacMillan's long-awaited *Anastasia* opens, with Seymour in the lead role. **4 August** The premiere of American choreographer Glen Tetley's contemporary ballet *Field Figures*.

1972 20 June Natalia Makarova dances Giselle, partnered by Dowell, making her debut at Covent Garden as a Guest Artist.

1973 8 June At Covent Garden, Nureyev and Makarova dance *The Sleeping Beauty* together for the first time.

1974 7 March Sibley, Dowell and David Wall dance the opening night of MacMillan's *Manon*. **7 October** The premiere of MacMillan's *Elite Syncopations* with Wayne Sleep in the Principal Character role.

1975 April The Royal Ballet makes its first tour of the Far East.

1976 12 February The first performance of Ashton's *A Month in the Country*, with Dowell and Seymour.

1977 13 June Norman Morrice succeeds MacMillan as Director of The Royal Ballet.

1978 14 February The premiere of MacMillan's full-length ballet *Mayerling*, the Principal male role created for David Wall.

1980s

1980 13 March MacMillan's *Gloria* receives its premiere. **4 August** Ashton creates *Rhapsody* for Lesley Collier and Mikhail Baryshnikov, given at a performance for the 80th birthday of HM Queen Elizabeth The Queen Mother.

1981 30 April World premiere of MacMillan's *Isadora* with Merle Park in the title role, to celebrate the Company's golden jubilee.

1982 2 December The premiere of Nureyev's *The Tempest*.

1984 24 February MacMillan's *Different Drummer* is created for the Company. **20 December** Collier and Dowell perform in the first night of Peter Wright's Biedermeier-inspired production of *The Nutcracker*.

1986 Anthony Dowell is appointed Director of The Royal Ballet.

1987 12 March *Swan Lake*, with Cynthia Harvey and Jonathan Cope, is Dowell's first production as Director. **16 December** Ashton stages a revival of *Cinderella*, his final production for The Royal Ballet.

1988 9 March Bintley's *'Still Life' at the Penguin Café* receives its world premiere with the Company. **19 August** Ashton dies in the year in which his *Ondine* is revived by Dowell after an absence of 22 years from the repertory.

1989 18 May The full-length *La Bayadère* is given its premiere by The Royal Ballet in a new production by Makarova. **8 December** MacMillan's final, full-evening production, *The Prince of the Pagodas*, is created for the Company, with Darcey Bussell and Jonathan Cope.

1990s

1990 19 July MacMillan's 'Farewell' *pas de deux* with Bussell and Irek Mukhamedov is performed at a London Palladium gala.

1991 7 February The first night of MacMillan's *Winter Dreams* (which grew out of the 'Farewell' *pas de deux*). **2 May** In celebration of the 60th anniversary of the Company, Bintley's *Cyrano* is first performed at a Royal Gala.

1992 13 February William Forsythe's *In the middle, somewhat elevated* is first performed by the Company. **19 March** MacMillan's last work, *The Judas Tree*, created for Mukhamedov and Viviana Durante, receives its premiere. **29 October** MacMillan dies of a heart attack during the first performance of a major revival of his *Mayerling*. **6 December** Ashton's *Tales of Beatrix Potter* is first staged by The Royal Ballet.

1993 7 April Baryshnikov's *Don Quixote* is first performed by the Company in new designs.

1994 6 April A new production of *The Sleeping Beauty* by Anthony Dowell is performed in Washington in the presence of the President of the USA and HRH The Princess Margaret. **18 June** Ashley Page's *Fearful Symmetries* is first performed (receiving the 1995 Olivier Award for Best New Dance Production). **3 November** Dowell's production of *The Sleeping Beauty* with designs by Maria Björnson is first performed at the Royal Opera House for a Royal Gala.

1996 2 May MacMillan's *Anastasia* is performed with new sets and costumes by Bob Crowley.

1997 14 July Farewell Gala and final performance at the 'old' Royal Opera House. During the closure The Royal Ballet is 'on tour', performing at Labatt's Apollo, Hammersmith, the Royal Festival Hall and the Barbican.

1999 December The redeveloped Royal Opera House opens. The Royal Ballet's first programme is 'A Celebration of International Choreography'. **17 December** The opening night of *The Nutcracker* is the first performance of a full-length ballet in the new House.

2000s

2000 8 February Revival of De Valois' production of *Coppélia* in the original designs by Osbert Lancaster opens. **29 February** Ashton's *Marguerite and Armand* is revived with Sylvie Guillem and Nicolas Le Riche in the title roles. **6 May** Millicent Hodson and Kenneth Archer produce a major restaging of Nijinsky's *Jeux* in a programme with *L'Après-midi d'un faune.*

2001 8 March De Valois dies. **July** Dowell retires as Director of The Royal Ballet. **23 October** The first performance of Nureyev's version of *Don Quixote* by The Royal Ballet, which marks the first performance under Ross Stretton's tenure as Director. **22 November** The first performance by The Royal Ballet of Cranko's *Onegin.*

2002 9 February HRH The Princess Margaret, Countess of Snowdon, President of The Royal Ballet, dies. **September** Ross Stretton resigns as Director. **December** Monica Mason becomes Director of the Company.

2003 13 January The Company dances Jiří Kylián's *Sinfonietta* for the first time. **8 March** The premiere of Makarova's new production of *The Sleeping Beauty*. **22 December** Wendy Ellis Somes's new production of *Cinderella* receives its premiere.

2004 April The Royal Ballet pays homage to Sergey Diaghilev in a 75th-anniversary tribute programme that includes the Company premiere of *Le Spectre de la rose*. **4 November** The premiere of Ashton's full-length *Sylvia*, reconstructed and staged by Christopher Newton for the 'Ashton 100' celebrations.

2005 7 May The premiere of a new work by Christopher Bruce, inspired by the life of Jimi Hendrix: *Three Songs – Two Voices.*

2006 15 May The Company begins its 75th-anniversary celebrations with a new production of the 1946 *Sleeping Beauty*, realized by Monica Mason and Christopher Newton with Messel's original designs, re-created by Peter Farmer, followed by revivals of Ashton's *Homage to The Queen*, with additional new choreography by Christopher Wheeldon, Michael Corder and David Bintley, and De Valois' *The Rake's Progress*. **8 June** A gala performance of *Homage* preceded by *La Valse* and *divertissements* is attended by HM The Queen. **November** The premieres of Wayne McGregor's *Chroma* and Wheeldon's *DGV: Danse à grande vitesse.* **December** McGregor becomes Resident Choreographer of The Royal Ballet.

2007 March Alastair Marriott's *Children of Adam* receives its premiere. **April** Will Tuckett's *The Seven Deadly Sins* receives its premiere. **June** Barry Wordsworth is appointed Music Director. **8 June** Darcey Bussell retires as a Principal. **23 November** The Royal Ballet performs Balanchine's *Jewels* in its entirety for the first time.

2008 28 February The first performance of Wheeldon's *Electric Counterpoint.* **23 April** The mainstage choreographic debut of Kim Brandstrup with *Rushes: Fragments of a Lost Story.* **15 June-21 July** The Royal Ballet goes on tour in China and the Far East, performing in Beijing, Shanghai, Tokyo, Osaka and Hong Kong. **October** marks the 50th anniversary of Ashton's *Ondine.* **13 November** The premiere of McGregor's *Infra.* **28 December** The Royal Ballet's first live cinema broadcast – *The Nutcracker* with Alexandra Ansanelli and Valeri Hristov.

2009 March Anthony Russell Roberts retires as Artistic Administrator and is succeeded by Kevin O'Hare. **April** Jeanetta Laurence is appointed Associate Director of The Royal Ballet. **June–July** The Royal Ballet tours to Washington D.C., Granada and Havana. **4 November** Wayne McGregor's *Limen* receives its premiere in a mixed programme with Glen Tetley's *Sphinx*, which enters the repertory for the first time. **17 November** A service to dedicate a memorial to the founders of The Royal Ballet is held at Westminster Abbey.

2010s

2010 January 50th anniversary of Ashton's *La Fille mal gardée.* **19 February** Main stage choreographic debut of Royal Ballet First Artist Jonathan Watkins with *As One.* **23 April** Miyako Yoshida dances her last performance with the Company at the Royal Opera House as Cinderella. **5 May** Main stage choreographic debut of Liam Scarlett with *Asphodel Meadows.*

Sarah Lamb as the Raven Girl and Thiago Soares as the Doctor in McGregor's *Raven Girl*

June–July The Royal Ballet tours to Japan for the tenth time (Tokyo and Osaka) and Spain (Barcelona). **29 June** Miyako Yoshida retires from the Company. **15 October** World Premiere of Brandstrup's *Invitus Invitam*.

2011 28 February World Premiere of Wheeldon's *Alice's Adventures in Wonderland*. **13 May** World Premiere of McGregor's *Live Fire Exercise*. **June–July** The Royal Ballet tours to Taiwan. **17-19 June** The Company appears at The O_2 Arena for the first time performing MacMillan's *Romeo and Juliet*.

2012 23 March The first 'Royal Ballet Live' is broadcast on the internet. **5 April** World Premiere of McGregor's *Carbon Life* and Scarlett's *Sweet Violets*. **2 June** MacMillan's *The Prince of the Pagodas* returns to the repertory after an absence of 16 years. **15–20 June** *Metamorphosis: Titian 2012*. **16 June** BP Big Screen. **20 June** Monica Mason retires as Director, succeeded by Kevin O'Hare. **30 October** HM The Queen's Diamond Jubilee is celebrated in a gala performance. **2 November** Liam Scarlett is appointed The Royal Ballet's first Artist in Residence.

2013 22 February World Premieres of Ratmansky's *24 Preludes* and Wheeldon's *Aeternum*. **February/March** A group from The Royal Ballet travels to Brazil for gala performances and to attend a symposium on dance in education. **8 May** World Premiere of Scarlett's *Hansel and Gretel*. **24 May** World Premiere of McGregor's *Raven Girl*. **27 May** Pita's *The Metamorphosis* is broadcast on Sky Arts. **June** The Royal Ballet tours to Monte Carlo. **20 June** World premiere of Kim Brandstrup's *Ceremony of Innocence* at the Aldeburgh Festival. **July** The Royal Ballet tours to Japan (Tokyo). **5 October** World Premiere of Carlos Acosta's *Don Quixote*. **9 November** World Premiere of David Dawson's *The Human Seasons*.

2014 7 February World Premiere of McGregor's *Tetractys – The Art of Fugue*. **10 April** World Premiere of Wheeldon's *The Winter's Tale*. **May** 50th anniversary of Ashton's *The Dream*. **31 May** World Premiere of Marriott's *Connectome*. **June** The Royal Ballet tours to the Bolshoi Theatre, Moscow, Taipei and Shanghai.

PRINCIPAL GUEST ARTIST

PRINCIPALS

Carlos Acosta
Joined as Principal 1998
Principal Guest Artist 2003
Born: Havana, Cuba
Trained: National Ballet School of Cuba
Previous Companies: English National Ballet (1991), National Ballet of Cuba (1992), Houston Ballet (1993)

Federico Bonelli
Joined as Principal 2003
Born: Genoa, Italy
Trained: Turin Dance Academy
Previous Companies: Zurich Ballet (1996), Dutch National Ballet (1999)

Lauren Cuthbertson
Joined 2002
Promoted to Principal 2008
Born: Devon, England
Trained: The Royal Ballet School

Matthew Golding
Joined as Principal 2014
Born: Sasketchewan, Canada
Trained: Royal Winnipeg Ballet, Universal Ballet Academy and The Royal Ballet School
Previous Companies: American Ballet Theatre (2003), Dutch National Ballet (2009)

Nehemiah Kish
Joined as Principal 2010
Born: Michigan, USA
Trained: National Ballet School of Canada
Previous Company: National Ballet of Canada (2001), Royal Danish Ballet (2008)

Sarah Lamb
Joined 2004
Promoted to Principal 2006
Born: Boston, USA
Trained: Boston Ballet School
Previous Company: Boston Ballet (1998)

Roberta Marquez
Joined and promoted to Principal 2004
Born: Rio de Janeiro, Brazil
Trained: Maria Olenewa State Dance School
Previous Company: Theatro Municipal, Rio de Janeiro (1994)

Steven McRae
Joined 2004
Promoted to Principal 2009
Born: Sydney, Australia
Trained: The Royal Ballet School

Laura Morera
Joined 1995
Promoted to Principal 2007
Born: Madrid, Spain
Trained:
The Royal Ballet School

Vadim Muntagirov
Joined as Principal 2014
Born: Chelyabinsk, Russia
Trained: Perm Choreographic Institute and The Royal Ballet School
Previous Company: English National Ballet (2009)

Marianela Nuñez
Joined 1998
Promoted to Principal 2002
Born: Buenos Aires
Trained:
Teatro Colón Ballet School, The Royal Ballet School

Natalia Osipova
Joined as Principal 2013
Born: Moscow
Trained: Bolshoi Ballet Academy
Previous Company: Bolshoi Ballet (2004), American Ballet Theatre (2010), Mikhailovsky Theatre (2011)

Rupert Pennefather
Joined 1999
Promoted to Principal 2008
Born: Maidenhead, England
Trained:
The Royal Ballet School

Thiago Soares
Joined 2002
Promoted to Principal 2006
Born: São Gonçalo, Brazil
Trained: Centre for Dance, Rio de Janeiro
Previous Company: Theatro Municipal, Rio de Janeiro (1998)

Edward Watson
Joined 1994
Promoted to Principal 2005
Born: Bromley, England
Trained:
The Royal Ballet School

Zenaida Yanowsky
Joined 1994
Promoted to Principal 2001
Born: Lyon, France
Trained: Las Palmas, Majorca
Previous Company: Paris Opéra Ballet (1994)

PRINCIPAL CHARACTER ARTISTS, CHARACTER ARTISTS, FIRST SOLOISTS AND SOLOISTS

PRINCIPAL CHARACTER ARTISTS
Left to right:
Gary Avis
Alastair Marriott
Elizabeth McGorian
Genesia Rosato

Christopher Saunders

CHARACTER ARTIST
Philip Mosley

FIRST SOLOISTS
Left to right:
Alexander Campbell
Ricardo Cervera
Deirdre Chapman
Yuhui Choe

Helen Crawford
Bennet Gartside
Melissa Hamilton
Ryoichi Hirano

Valeri Hristov
Hikaru Kobayashi
Itziar Mendizabal
Johannes Stepanek

Akane Takada
Valentino Zucchetti

SOLOISTS
Left to right:
Christina Arestis
Claire Calvert

Olivia Cowley
Tristan Dyer
Elizabeth Harrod
James Hay

Francesca Hayward
Jonathan Howells
Fumi Kaneko
Paul Kay

SOLOISTS, FIRST ARTISTS AND ARTISTS

Emma Maguire
Laura McCulloch
Kristen McNally
Fernando Montaño

Yasmine Naghdi
Beatriz Stix-Brunell
Eric Underwood
Thomas Whitehead

FIRST ARTISTS
Left to right:
Luca Acri
Tara-Brigitte Bhavnani
Jacqueline Clark
Leanne Cope

Nicol Edmonds
Kevin Emerton
Hayley Forskitt
Elsa Godard

Nathalie Harrison

Meaghan Grace Hinkis

Pietra Mello-Pittman

Erico Montes

Sian Murphy

Romany Pajdak

Gemma Pitchley-Gale

Marcelino Sambé

Michael Stojko

Lara Turk

Andrej Uspenski

James Wilkie

ARTISTS
Left to right:

Matthew Ball

Sander Blommaert

Camille Bracher

Annette Buvoli

Reece Clarke
David Donnelly
Téo Dubreuil
Benjamin Ella

Isabella Gasparini
Solomon Golding
Hannah Grennell
Tierney Heap

Mayara Magri
Tomas Mock
Anna Rose O'Sullivan
Demelza Parish

Calvin Richardson
Mariko Sasaki
Leticia Stock
Gina Storm-Jensen

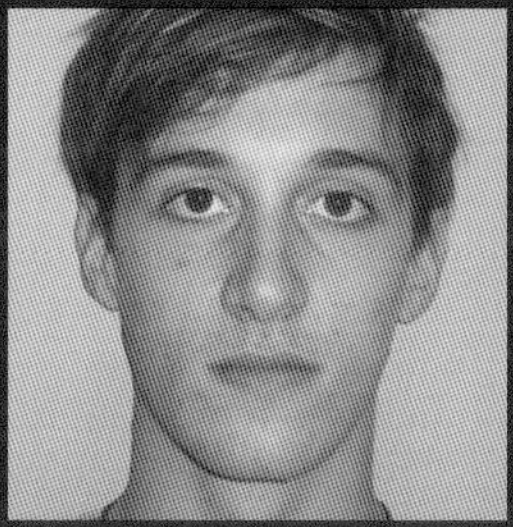

Donald Thom

PRIX DE LAUSANNE DANCER

David Yudes

AUD JEBSEN YOUNG DANCERS PROGRAMME

Left to right:

Maria Barroso

Grace Blundell

Grace Horler

Ashleigh McKimmie

Ashley Scott

Left to right:

Artistic Associate
Christopher Wheeldon

Associate Director
Jeanetta Laurence

Director
Kevin O'Hare

Resident Choreographer
Wayne McGregor

Music Director
Barry Wordsworth

©Elliott Franks

THE ROYAL BALLET 2014/15

Patron HM The Queen
President HRH The Prince of Wales
Vice-President The Lady Sarah Chatto

Director††† Kevin O'Hare
Associate Director Jeanetta Laurence

Music Director Barry Wordsworth
Resident Choreographer Wayne McGregor CBE
Artistic Associate Christopher Wheeldon

General Manager
Heather Baxter

Company Manager and Tour Manager
Andrew Hurst

Artistic Scheduling Manager and Character Artist
Philip Mosley

Financial Controller
Cathy Helweg

Contracts Administrator
Alison Tedbury

Deputy Company Manager
Elizabeth Ferguson

Assistant to the Directors and Artistic Co-ordinator (maternity cover)
Daniel Siekhaus

Administrative Co-ordinator
Yvonne Hunte

Management Accountant
Orsola Ricciardelli

Clinical Director, Ballet Healthcare
Gregory Retter

Head of Physiotherapy and Chartered Physiotherapist
Moira McCormack

Chartered Physiotherapist
Daniel Watson

Body Control Instructors
Jane Paris
Fiona Kleckham

Occupational Psychologist
Britt Tajet-Foxell

Masseurs
Tatina Semprini
Konrad Simpson
Helen Wellington

Sports Science
Patrick Rump
Frank Appel
Brian Maloney

Consultant Orthopaedic Surgeon
R Lloyd Williams

Medical Advisor
Ian Beasley

Healthcare Team Assistant
Olivia Powell

Senior Ballet Master
Christopher Saunders

Ballet Master
Gary Avis

Ballet Mistress
Samantha Raine

Assistant Ballet Master
Ricardo Cervera
Jonathan Howells

Assistant Ballet Mistress
Laura McCulloch

Senior Teacher and Répétiteur to the Principal Artists
Alexander Agadzhanov

Répétiteurs
Lesley Collier
Jonathan Cope

Senior Notator
Anna Trevien

Notator
Gregory Mislin

Education Administrator and Teacher
David Pickering

Artist in Residence
Liam Scarlett

Head of Music Staff
Robert Clark

Music Staff
Richard Coates
Philip Cornfield
Craig Edwards
Grant Green
Tim Qualtrough
Kate Shipway
Paul Stobart

Music Administrator
Nigel Bates

Studio Programme Senior Producer
Emma Southworth

Producer
Poppy Ben David

Administrative Co-ordinator
Hannah Mayhew

Guest Principal Ballet Master
Christopher Carr

Principal Guest Teacher
Elizabeth Anderton

Guest Teachers
Boris Akimov
Jacquelin Barrett
Johnny Eliasen
Olga Evreinoff
Antonia Franceschi
Andrey Klemm
Alessandra Pasquali
Roland Price
Matz Skoog

Conductors
David Briskin
Dominic Grier
Boris Gruzin
Koen Kessels
Emmanuel Plasson
Tom Seligman
Barry Wordsworth
Martin Yates

Principals
Carlos Acosta†
Roberto Bolle††
Federico Bonelli
Lauren Cuthbertson
Matthew Golding
Nehemiah Kish
Sarah Lamb
Roberta Marquez
Steven McRae
Laura Morera
Vadim Muntagirov
Marianela Nuñez
Evgenia Obraztsova††
Natalia Osipova
Rupert Pennefather
Iana Salenko††
Thiago Soares
Edward Watson
Zenaida Yanowsky

Principal Character Artists
Gary Avis
Alastair Marriott
Elizabeth McGorian
Genesia Rosato
Christopher Saunders
William Tuckett††

First Soloists
Alexander Campbell
Ricardo Cervera
Deirdre Chapman
Yuhui Choe
Helen Crawford
Bennet Gartside
Melissa Hamilton
Ryoichi Hirano
Valeri Hristov
Hikaru Kobayashi
Itziar Mendizabal
Johannes Stepanek
Akane Takada
Valentino Zucchetti

Soloists
Christina Arestis
Claire Calvert
Olivia Cowley
Tristan Dyer
Elizabeth Harrod
James Hay
Francesca Hayward
Jonathan Howells
Fumi Kaneko
Paul Kay
Emma Maguire
Laura McCulloch
Kristen McNally
Fernando Montaño
Yasmine Naghdi
Beatriz Stix-Brunell
Eric Underwood
Thomas Whitehead

First Artists
Luca Acri
Tara-Brigitte Bhavnani
Jacqueline Clark
Leanne Cope
Nicol Edmonds
Kevin Emerton
Hayley Forskitt
Elsa Godard
Nathalie Harrison
Meaghan Grace Hinkis
Pietra Mello-Pittman
Erico Montes
Sian Murphy
Romany Pajdak
Gemma Pitchley-Gale
Marcelino Sambé
Michael Stojko
Lara Turk
Andrej Uspenski
James Wilkie

Artists
Matthew Ball
Sander Blommaert
Camille Bracher
Annette Buvoli
Reece Clarke
David Donnelly
Téo Dubreuil
Benjamin Ella
Isabella Gasparini
Solomon Golding
Hannah Grennell
Tierney Heap
Mayara Magri
Tomas Mock
Anna Rose O'Sullivan
Demelza Parish
Calvin Richardson
Mariko Sasaki
Leticia Stock
Gina Storm-Jensen
Donald Thom

Prix de Lausanne dancer
David Yudes

Aud Jebsen Young Dancers Programme
Maria Barroso
Grace Blundell
Grace Horler
Ashleigh McKimmie
Ashley Scott

† Principal Guest Artist
†† Guest Artist
††† Position generously supported by Lady Ashcroft

Governors of the Royal Ballet Companies

Chairman
Dame Jenny Abramsky DBE

Professor Michael Clarke CBE DL
Ricki Gail Conway
The Marchioness of Douro OBE
Dame Vivien Duffield DBE
Stephen Hough
Desmond Kelly OBE
Thomas Lynch
Gail Monahan
Christopher Nourse
Marguerite Porter
Simon Robey
Dame Sue Street DCB
Monica Zamora

Honorary Secretary
Peter Wilson

In 1956 Queen Elizabeth II granted the then Sadler's Wells Ballet, Sadler's Wells Theatre Ballet and Sadler's Wells School a Royal Charter, and they became respectively The Royal Ballet and Royal Ballet School. Under the Charter a body of Governors was set up whose ultimate duty it is to safeguard the future of the Company (now The Royal Ballet and Birmingham Royal Ballet) and School and to be the custodians of the traditions established by Dame Ninette de Valois in the formation of the Company and School in 1931.

SELECTED BOOKS ABOUT THE ROYAL BALLET AND ITS DANCERS

Dancers: Behind the Scenes with The Royal Ballet

By Andrej Uspenski

This beautifully produced book by Royal Ballet dancer Andrej Uspenski is a collection of exclusive photographs which shines the spotlight on ballet, the most beautiful of art forms. These exquisite photographs feature some of the finest dancers on stage today, bringing the reader into the magical world of ballet. As a Royal Ballet dancer himself, Andrej Uspenski has a unique perspective on the photographic composition of dance imagery, as well as unrivalled access not only to The Royal Ballet's productions, but also to the dancers who perform in them. This gives the reader an exclusive insight into The Royal Ballet's work. *Dancers* includes exclusive, backstage photographs, as well as a number of breathtaking images taken from the wings during live stage performances, making this a unique photographic record, perfect for all ballet fans. Oberon Books, 2013

ISBN 978-1-84943-388-4

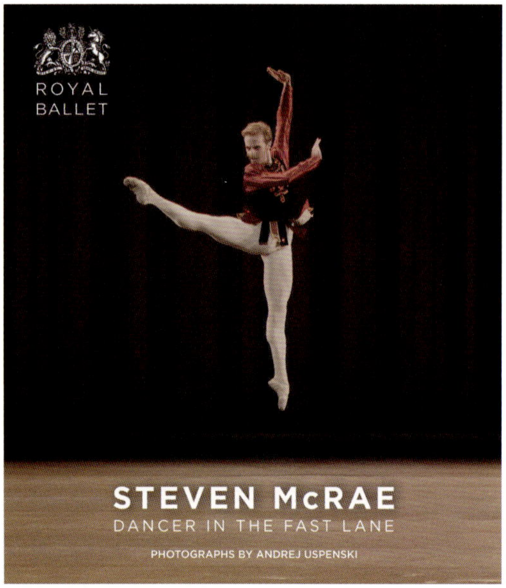

Steven McRae – Dancer in the Fast Lane

By Andrej Uspenski

Steven McRae: Dancer in the Fast Lane is a collection of photographs of Royal Ballet Principal Steven McRae. Photographer and Royal Ballet dancer Andrej Uspenski has once again used his exclusive vantage point to capture glimpses of Steven on stage and in rehearsal, for both classic and contemporary work with The Royal Ballet. Introduced by Steven McRae, and including images of Steven rehearsing Kenneth MacMillan's *Romeo and Juliet* with Guest Principal Evgenia Obraztsova. Oberon Books, 2014.

ISBN 978-1-78319-088-1

Natalia Osipova: Becoming a Swan

By Andrej Uspenski

Natalia Osipova: Becoming A Swan is an intimate portrait of the work of Royal Ballet Principal Natalia Osipova. This story of a dancer preparing for the most iconic role in ballet, behind the scenes and on stage, with unique glimpses from the wings at the Royal Opera House, is told in more than 150 black and white images by Royal Ballet dancer Andrej Uspenski. This is a moving photographic tribute to one of the world's most exciting ballerinas. Foreword by Alexander Agadzhanov, The Royal Ballet's Senior Teacher and Répétiteur to the Principal Artists. Oberon Books, 2013.

ISBN 978-1-78319-022-5

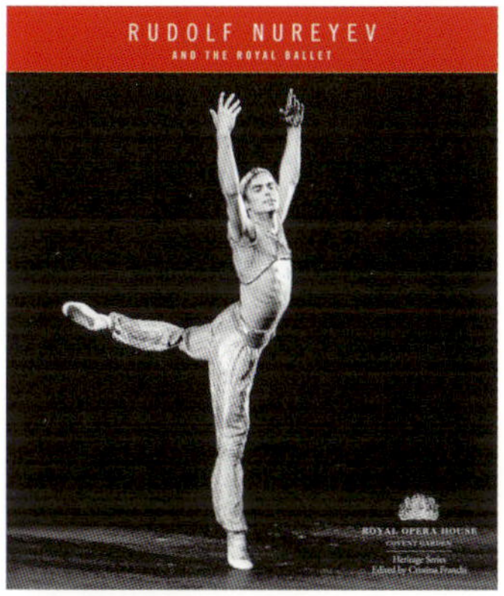

Rudolf Nureyev and The Royal Ballet

Black and white photographs documenting Rudolf Nureyev's long association with The Royal Ballet, edited by Cristina Franchi. Oberon Books, 2005

ISBN 978-1-84002-462-3

Margot Fonteyn: Prima Ballerina Assoluta of The Royal Ballet

Black and white photographs documenting Margot Fonteyn's long association with The Royal Ballet, edited by Cristina Franchi. Oberon Books, 2004

ISBN 978-1-84002-460-9

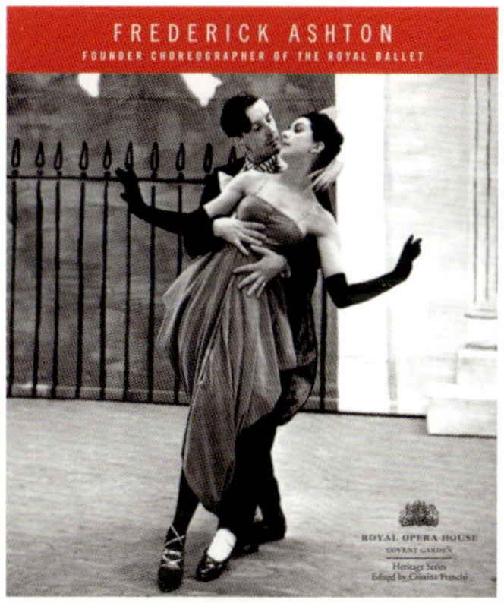

Frederick Ashton: Founder Choreographer of The Royal Ballet

Black and white photographs documenting Frederick Ashton's career and works made for The Royal Ballet, edited by Cristina Franchi. Oberon Books, 2004

ISBN 978-1-84002-461-6

Royal Opera House Souvenir Guide

Explore the Royal Opera House, its history, performance, architecture and backstage. Oberon Books, 2012

ISBN 978-1-84943-167-5

Pas de deux: The Royal Ballet in Pictures

More than two hundred stunning colour and black and white photographs of The Royal Ballet in rehearsal and performance. This is a unique photographic record of one of the foremost ballet companies in the world in performance and rehearsal at the Royal Opera House. Oberon Books, 2007

ISBN 978-1-84002-777-8

Royal Ballet Yearbook 2013/14

The new edition for the 2013/14 season will bring all ballet lovers up to date with the latest activities, performances and company news from the prestigious Royal Ballet. Featuring lavish photographs of last Season's performances, a special preview of the new Season and lively and informative articles, the Yearbook is a richly illustrated companion to The Royal Ballet, its history, repertory, dancers and staff. Oberon Books, 2013

ISBN 978-1-78319-002-7

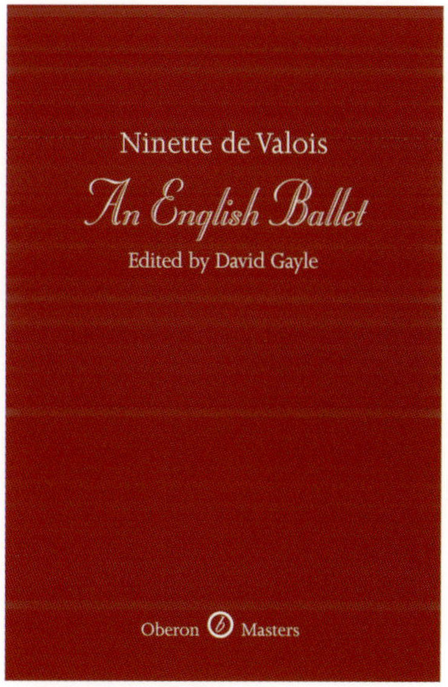

An English Ballet

By Ninette de Valois
Edited by David Gayle

Historic talk and essay from the Founder of The Royal Ballet. Oberon Books, 2011

ISBN 978-1-84943-107-1

ISBN 978-1-78319-081-2

9 781783 190812 >

OBERON BOOKS
www.oberonbooks.com